THE OLD STONE FORT

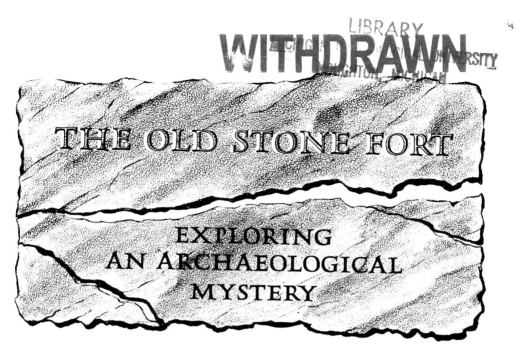

THE OLD STONE FORT

EXPLORING AN ARCHAEOLOGICAL MYSTERY

BY CHARLES H. FAULKNER

A University of Tennessee Study in Anthropology

THE UNIVERSITY OF TENNESSEE PRESS: KNOXVILLE

Library of Congress Catalog Card Number 68–17145
International Standard Book Number 0–87049–086–9
Manufactured in the United States of America

✍ PREFACE: A HISTORIC SITE ✍

with a note to the second printing

Lᴏᴄᴀʟ ʟᴇɢᴇɴᴅs, fostered by the absence of factual knowledge, have for years given an aura of mystery to the Tennessee site known popularly as the Old Stone Fort. Located in Coffee County near the town of Manchester, the sprawling rock and earth enclosure has at various times been attributed to the work of Norsemen, early Welshmen, or one of several prehistoric American Indian tribes. And because the nature of mystery lends itself to speculation, guesses have also been offered about what the Old Stone Fort was used for and when it was actually constructed.

Beyond the fact that the structure existed when white men first settled the area, little was known about either its function or the date of its construction. The prevalent belief was that it was a fort, a defensive structure used by someone for protection. An alternate theory, scarcely given credence until the 20th century, was that the structure might have had some specific ceremonial function. The fact that Norsemen were considered as possible builders implies a belief that the Old Stone Fort was standing before Columbus discovered the New World.

Lending additional local interest to the site has been the record of its use since the late 18th century when the soldiers of the Nickajack Expedition, sent against the Chickamauga Cherokee towns in 1794, camped within its walls (Davidson, 1946: 195–96). The route taken by the invading army was along an old Indian trail that passed near the Old Stone Fort. This site again became an army bivouac in 1863 when Federal troops moved south along this route from Nashville to Chattanooga after the battle of Stone's River (Murfreesboro). Present U.S. 41 from Nashville to Chattanooga approximately follows these historically significant routes.

The proximity of this site to the established route through Middle Tennessee and to water power resources of the forks of the Duck River made it an important industrial center at an early date. Ewell says that in 1823 a rope factory was built at the falls of the Little Duck River and that after this building was destroyed by fire in 1847, a flour, grist, and sawmill was constructed on the same site. In 1852, a paper mill was erected on the Duck River proper near the south end of the Old Stone Fort. Ten years later, in 1862, a powder mill was built nearby to provide munitions for the Confederate army; but Union troops destroyed this powder source the following year. The last major industry at the site was the Stone Fort Paper Company, which was built at the Big Falls of the Duck River in 1879 (Ewell, 1936: 35).

On April 23, 1966, the state of Tennessee took the first step to preserve this important historic site when it was included in a purchase of four hundred acres of land of the John Chumbley estate on which to develop a state park. The state immediately engaged the University of Tennessee's Department of Anthropology to conduct research in an attempt to discover the builders, age, and function of the Old Stone Fort before reconstruction of the site was initiated. The University department carried out its investigation during midsummer of that same year.

A NOTE TO THE SECOND PRINTING

ARCHAEOLOGICAL exploration is a continuous, tedious process. Time and the elements erect many subtle barriers to hide man's past from the prying eyes of archaeologists. The mystery of the people who built the Old Stone Fort is no exception, but the clues to their origin are slowly being sifted. Since this book was first published, two discoveries concerning the builders of this enclosure have confirmed our earlier predictions.

Although the existence of stone mounds (Jones, 1876:103) has yet to be positively established, a recent reconnaissance has revealed a low earth mound east of the enclosure on a heavily wooded terrace of the Little Duck River. Only about 30 feet in diameter and less than three feet high, the mound is similar in configuration to prehistoric mounds in this part of the state, but only excavation will reveal its actual origin.

Probably the most important discovery has been the habitation sites of Middle Woodland Indians who built the Old Stone Fort. The author and members of the Coffee-Franklin County Chapter of the Tennessee Archaeological Society have located at least five Middle Woodland habitation sites within 20 miles of the enclosure. None of these sites are in the immediate vicinity of the fort, but the largest is only about three miles downstream (one linear mile) and appears to have been an intensively occupied village. The predominant projectile point found at this site is triangular, similar to the Middle Woodland Copena point of northern Alabama. The complicated stamped pottery as well as the limestone-tempered plain and check stamped ceramics are the same types found on Middle Woodland sites in the eastern Tennessee Valley and Copena sites in Alabama. Other typical Middle Woodland artifacts found on the surface here include gorgets and greenstone celts. A smaller site nearby produced a fragment of what appears to be a large steatite pipe resembling the one in Plate 6. There seems to be little doubt that these habitation sites were occupied by the Indians who built the Old Stone Fort. Their distance from the fort also supports the contention that this structure served as a ceremonial center for a widely scattered population in the upper Duck Valley.

As the Old Stone Fort State Park is developed, it is hoped that this important archaeological site will continue to reveal its secrets, particularly what motivated this group of Indians to build such a large, impressive structure of apparently non-utilitarian purpose.

ACKNOWLEDGMENTS

The AUTHOR wishes to express his gratitude to all those who aided him in this project. Donald M. McSween, Commissioner, and Walter L. Criley, Director, Division of Planning, Tennessee Department of Conservation, helped make the project a reality. Paul Russell, United States Department of Agriculture, surveyed the entrance complex, and his help was indispensable in mapping this portion of the site.

Grady York and Carey Waldrip, two citizens of Manchester whose interest in the Old Stone Fort has been rewarded by the development of plans for a state park at this site, deserve thanks for their helpfulness during the excavation. Their interest and friendliness were typical of the residents of Manchester.

The project was directed by Alfred K. Guthe, Head of the University of Tennessee's Department of Anthropology. J. B. Graham served as field supervisor; he and the ten student crew-members should be especially cited for their industry and patience, since it often seemed that the moving of tons of rock would yield little that could be interpreted. The information contained in this report is testimony of their diligence.

Members of the crew who also served as field and laboratory assistants include Stanley Ahler, Brian Butler, and Carey Oakley. Stan Ahler deserves special recognition for processing the artifacts found in the field and for his assistance in drawing the entrance-way map. The tables and plates were prepared by J. B. Graham, and figures were drawn by Beve Lea Teasley.

Special thanks go also to Helen Orton Williams, St. Louis artist, whose conception of the entranceway to the Old Stone Fort appears as Figure 8, and to the University of Tennessee Photographic Service for the photographs appearing as Plates 3, 4, 5, 7, and 12. Our competent secretary, Miss Janette Starkey, typed the manuscript.

The original manuscript prepared for the Tennessee Department of Conservation was read and commented upon by Raymond S. Baby, Ohio State Museum; Carl H. Chapman, University of Missouri; James E. Fitting, Case Western Reserve University; James B. Griffin, University of Michigan; Martha A. Potter, Ohio State Museum; and Stuart Struever, Northwestern University. The author is deeply grateful for their professional advice and constructive criticisms. Any errors of fact or interpretation are entirely his own responsibility.

C.H.F.
Knoxville, 1971

✎ CONTENTS ✎

ILLUSTRATIONS

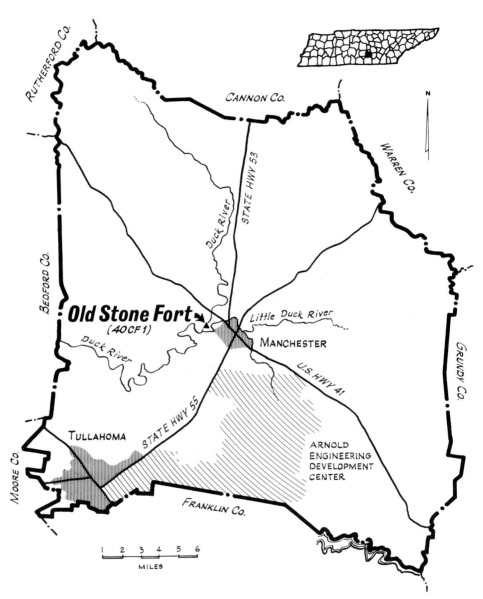

Figure 1: Location of Site, Coffee County, Tennessee

⤳ THE SETTING ⤶

THE OLD STONE FORT is located in the south-central part of Tennessee on the outskirts of Manchester, which is the county seat of Coffee County and near its center (Figure 1). Geographically, this is the state's Highland Rim section, a part of the Interior Low Plateau province,[1] and it is characterized by level to moderately steep topography averaging 1,050 feet above sea level.

Most of the Highland Rim section is known locally as the "Barrens," perhaps getting this name from the generally unproductive soil that is derived from the underlying formation of Fort Payne chert. Large portions of the Barrens were said to be devoid of trees and covered only with underbrush and cane when the first settlers arrived. Since drainage of the Barrens is not well developed, the area of the Old Stone Fort provides an important topographic feature: the Barrens' only pronounced stream dissection is near this site where the Duck River and its tributaries flow through deep gorges.

Mention of the Old Stone Fort in area history is frequent. It has been described since the early 19th century, and maps of the structure have appeared periodically in writings about the antiquities of Tennessee (see Plates 1 and 2). If all accounts had agreed about the appearance of the enclosure, and if portions of its walls had not been removed, reconstruction would have been a relatively simple task. However, these early maps and descriptions often proved to be dissimilar, and time and destruction took their toll on the walls.

Fortunately, the walls were substantial enough to generally with-

[1] The major source for the geographic setting of the Old Stone Fort is Love et al., 1959.

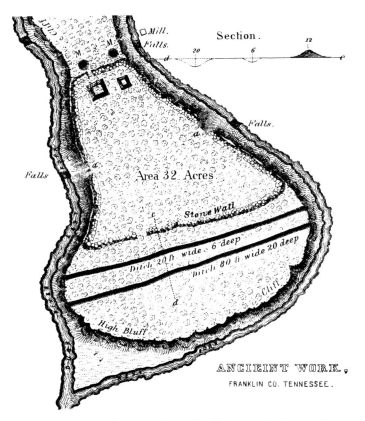

Section.

Mill.
Falls.
20   6   12

Falls.

Falls

Area 32 Acres

Stone Wall

Ditch 20 ft wide 6 deep

Ditch 80 ft wide 20 deep

Cliff

High Bluff

ANCIENT WORK,
FRANKLIN CO. TENNESSEE.

Plate 1: Old Stone Fort (Squire and Davis, 1848).

stand the rigors of time, allowing observers of the 19th century
to describe the Old Stone Fort's over-all appearance. Nearly all
reports agree that it is an enclosure of rock and earth walls, impressive in size and engineering, and built on the end of a natural
plateau where the two forks of the Duck River converge (see
Figure 2). Before the two streams meet below this plateau, they
flow through deep gorges cut in Paleozoic rocks. The upper formation in the gorges is the Mississippian Fort Payne, which includes hard, bedded chert and calcareous and dolomitic silicastones.
The hard rocks in this formation are found in a series of erosion-
resistant beds over which the streams flow in rapids and water-
falls (see Plate 3). Below the Fort Payne formation is the softer

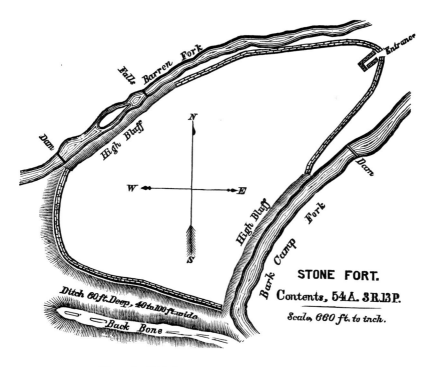

Plate 2: Old Stone Fort (Jones, 1876).

Chattanooga shale. The chunks of chert and slabs of black shale scattered along the stream beds were used to construct the walls of the Old Stone Fort.

Encircling an area of fifty acres, the walls, if they were continuous, would have a total length of about 4,600 feet. However, they are not continuous; they were constructed only where the stream bluffs were not steep. For simplicity the walls can be designated by the cardinal points (north, south, east, and west), although they are not actually aligned in those directions. The "north" wall is not separate; it consists of the north ends of the "east" and "west" walls where they converge to form a cul-de-sac entranceway. Since the length of the north wall is arbitrary, it is included in the measurements of the east and west walls. From the north entranceway, the east and west walls angle toward and then follow the river bluffs until the bluffs become sheer cliffs 80 to 100

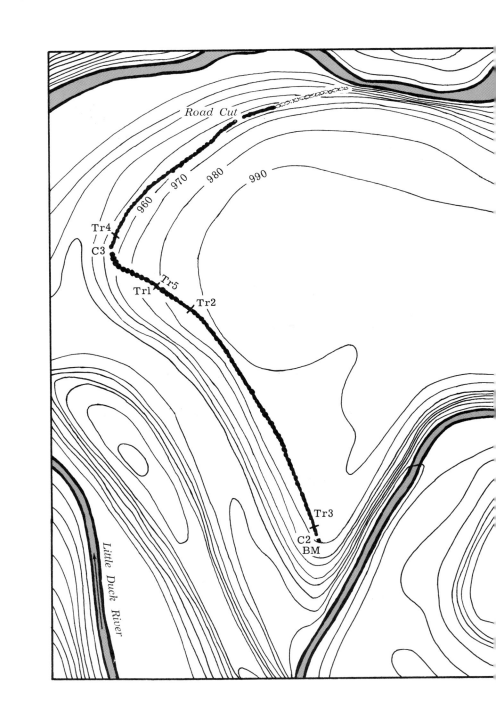

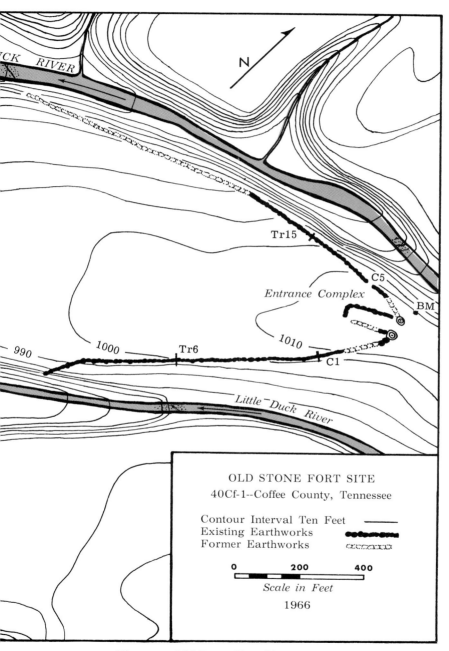

N

DUCK RIVER

Tr15

C5

BM

Entrance Complex

990 1000 Tr6 1010 C1

Little Duck River

OLD STONE FORT SITE
40Cf-1--Coffee County, Tennessee

Contour Interval Ten Feet ——————
Existing Earthworks ●●●●●●●●●●
Former Earthworks ⊂⊃⊂⊃⊂⊃⊂⊃

0   200   400
Scale in Feet
1966

Figure 2: Old Stone Fort Site

Plate 3: Falls on the Duck River on the west side of the Old Stone Fort.

feet high (see Plates 4 and 5). The existing and assumed portions of the east wall skirt the bluff of the Little Duck River (formerly called the Bark Camp Fork of the Duck River) for 1,094.7 feet. This distance includes the diameter (now 50 feet) of the east pedestal.[2] The west wall runs 1,396.4 feet (including the west pedestal and 810 feet of destroyed but traceable wall) from the entrance along the bluffs of the Duck River proper (formerly the Barren Fork). Like the east wall, this work ends where the bluffs become cliffs. On either side, walls do not reappear until the south end of the ridge is reached, where the stream bluffs have a more gentle

[2]The term "pedestal" is used to describe the two mounds on either side of the entranceway since these structures appear to be an actual part of the walls and not mounds constructed separately for burial or some other ceremonial function.

Plate 4: Bluffs on the west bank of the Duck River. The view is from the west side of the Old Stone Fort.

Plate 5: Bluffs along the Little Duck River below the east wall of the Old Stone Fort.

slope. Here the "south" wall was constructed from one stream to the other, a distance of 2,116.6 feet.

Although early descriptions of the walls are consistent in some ways, they disagree about the height and length of the walls, the material used to build them, the area they enclose, and, most of all, the appearance of the north entranceway. An examination of published accounts of the Old Stone Fort makes it obvious that many authors never visited the site; they based their descriptions on earlier accounts or even paraphrased what early eyewitnesses told them. Although Haywood (1823) and Squire and Davis (1848) give details about the enclosure, both works rely on earlier accounts. Haywood supposedly visited the site, but his description is very much like the description by William Donnison in the Boston *Columbian Centinel*, July 31, 1819. Squire and Davis relied on a plan by C. S. Rafinesque[3] that in turn closely corresponded to plans in the *Western Messenger* and to Haywood's 1823 description (Plate 1). Since Squire and Davis never actually visited the site, their account is of dubious value. Other eyewitness reports of the fort are on record, but the one that seems most accurate was published by Joseph Jones, who not only personally explored the site but also contracted with a resident of Manchester for a resurvey (Plate 2).

The 19th century was a century of speculation as far as the Old Stone Fort is concerned. It was not until 1928 that a careful scientific attempt was made to answer questions raised in the preceding century. In September of 1928, P. E. Cox, Tennessee State Archaeologist, spent two weeks excavating various parts of the Old Stone Fort walls and interior. Even then the major riddles about the fort—its age, its function, and the identity of its builders—were left unsolved. The 1966 University of Tennessee excavation provided at least partial answers to these puzzling questions.

[3]A volume of Rafinesque manuscripts is in the collection of the University of Pennsylvania Museum. Although Squire and Davis report the existence of two plans of the Old Stone Fort, a careful study of the Rafinesque manuscript revealed only the plan used by the English antiquarians. No date could be found on this particular drawing. The author would like to express his appreciation to Cynthia Griffin and Linton Satterthwaite for their study of the manuscript and for a copy of the Rafinesque sketch of the Old Stone Fort.

Builders of the Old Stone Fort

There is now little doubt that a prehistoric group of American Indians built the enclosure known as the Old Stone Fort.[4] Local legends giving Norsemen and the Welsh as builders are not based on fact, since there is no historical or archaeological evidence of European migrants in the southeastern interior of this continent during the first four or five centuries of the Christian Era.[5] A lack of contact between Europe and the Southeast at this time is almost universally accepted among professional archaeologists.

Although cultural material on this site is scarce, we now believe that the particular group of prehistoric people who built this structure was the Middle Woodland Indians, known to have lived in Tennessee shortly after the birth of Christ.

The Middle Woodland Indians are identified with one of four distinct periods into which the prehistory of Tennessee can be divided: the *Paleo-Indian* (12000–9000 B.C.), the *Archaic* (8000–1000 B.C.), the *Woodland* (1000 B.C.–A.D. 1000), and the *Mississippian* (A.D. 1000–European contact).[6] The earliest inhabitants of the state, the Paleo-Indians, roamed the land in search of game at the end of the last Ice Age. In the Archaic period, these roving

[4]Speculation once ranged from the Yuchi tribe, who supposedly dwelt within the walls during the 16th century when De Soto explored the Southeast, to the enigmatic "Mound Builders," prehistoric Indians who roamed Middle Tennessee as early as 2,000 years ago.

[5]Although the archaeological evidence proves the Indian origin of the Old Stone Fort, it would be an injustice to American literature not to footnote at least some of the attempts by historians to establish the presence of Europeans in the Southeast before Columbus' voyage to the New World. The most popular local legends concerning the builders of the fort are about wandering Norsemen in the 10th and 11th centuries A.D. and about a lost group of Welshmen under the leadership of Prince Madoc in the 12th century A.D. Although prehistorians have now firmly established that Viking seafarers sailed the eastern coast of North America before Columbus' voyage, the presence of Madoc and his followers has never been proved, despite recurring reports of blue-eyed Indians speaking a Celtic tongue. Perhaps one of the most imaginative theories about the builders of the fort concerns the Buccaneers of Seville who, the legend goes, landed on the coast of Florida and eventually made their way into the interior of the continent, where they built the Old Stone Fort to protect themselves from the unfriendly natives. All of these theories have been presented in considerable detail by Basil B. McMahan in *The Mystery of the Old Stone Fort*.

[6]The dates for these periods are approximations to aid the reader in understanding the time perspective and should not be construed as absolute.

hunters began to settle at favorable fishing and gathering sites. In the Woodland period, which embraced the builders of the Old Stone Fort, they first began to practice agriculture and to build burial mounds near their small villages; and in the fourth and final period the Indians of Tennessee became intensive farmers and built flat-topped mounds for temples and council houses in their large permanent villages.

These major periods are further subdivided into shorter units of time, characterized by the emergence or presence of distinct prehistoric cultures. In the case of the Woodland period, the divisions are "Early," "Middle," and "Late," and in Tennessee the Middle Woodland period spanned the first four or five centuries of the Christian Era. This period is notable for the florescence of the Hopewell culture in the Ohio region, a dynamic culture whose influence was felt in many local Middle Woodland cultures throughout eastern North America, including some in what is now the state of Tennessee.

An important fact in arriving at this designation of the probable builders is that the Old Stone Fort is not a unique structure in eastern North America. Stone and earth walls, in some cases constructed so as to suggest a defensive enclosure, are found in other areas of the East. Many are not as complex and impressive as the Tennessee work, and consequently have not received the attention they deserve, but their mere presence suggests a possible relationship to the Old Stone Fort. If a prehistoric group of people built such enclosures in another area, perhaps this same group was responsible for the Old Stone Fort. In eastern North America, the Ohio Valley and particularly the state of Ohio stand out as the center of prehistoric earth and stone construction. As early as 1848, Squire and Davis (p. 3) observed:

in the region watered by the Ohio and its tributaries, we find ancient works of greater magnitude and more manifest design. . . . Here we find numberless mounds, most of them conical but many pyramidal in form, and often of great dimensions. . . . Accompanying these, and in some instances sustaining an intimate relation to them, are numerous enclosures of earth and stone, frequently of vast size, and often of regular outline.

Squire and Davis' category of enclosures can be divided into two distinctive types: earthen walls around large groups of burial mounds in the river valleys, undoubtedly built to enclose a sacred area; and so-called hilltop enclosures or fortifications that are located on high hills or ridges above the river valleys. These hilltop enclosures sometimes enclose mounds but often contain no evidence of ceremony. The ceremonial function of the former type of enclosure has never been seriously questioned, but the apparently nonceremonial nature and strategic position of the latter have led numerous writers to call them "fortifications." The Old Stone Fort and other Southeastern enclosures seem to be of this second type.

Shortly after the turn of the century the builders of some of these enclosures had been identified as the Hopewell "people" (Mills, 1906: 135), who "were responsible for the erection of a score or more of imposing geometric earthworks and accompanying mounds scattered throughout southern Ohio and contiguous territory" (Shetrone, 1930: 187). Although Shetrone states that the builder of the hilltop enclosures or fortifications "is not definitely known" (1930: 223) and attributes the construction of Fort Ancient in Warren County, Ohio, to the later prehistoric culture that bears this site's name, North American archaeologists now agree that Fort Ancient and most comparable Ohio structures were built by the Hopewell culture (Morgan, 1946; Prufer, 1964).

More important than the similarity in configuration of the enclosures in the Southeast and the enclosures in the Ohio area is the fact that there are parallels in methods of construction. In both areas, rough stone was used for wall filler, flat slabs were placed at the base of the walls, and mounds or pillars were added. Also, what might be called "complex entranceways" were formed by ditches and inner walls.

The Fort Ancient earthwork in Warren County, Ohio, is certainly one of the most impressive examples of Hopewell building activity in the Ohio Valley. Although the walls of this enclosure, which vary from 4 to 23 feet in height, are composed mainly of earth (Morgan, 1946: 5), much stone was also used in their construction. Moorehead's monumental work (1890) elaborates several times on the use of stone. On page 18 Moorehead states, "At station 295, the wall is composed almost entirely of stone, which shows on the outer slope for fully 20 feet below the top." Later he describes what might be a pavement under the walls when he says, "There are large flat stones at the bottom of the wall at this point, and they crop out at the edges and can be plainly seen" (p. 22). His conclusions about the use of stone are "that the builders of the fort used stone throughout the entire length of the walls, save, it may be, where they were very low; and that the embankments have what we might name a *stone backbone*" (p. 90).

Several other hilltop enclosures in Ohio have stone incorporated into the walls. The Spruce Hill enclosure in Ross County has walls consisting almost entirely of stone (Squire and Davis, 1848: 11; Fowke, 1902: 242). In Butler County, a work known as "Fortified Hill" surrounds an area of about sixteen acres. Squire and Davis describe the wall as "of mingled earth and stone . . . the earth composing it . . . is a stiff clay" (1848: 17). Fort Hill, a well-known site in Highland County on the summit of a high point, consists of an embankment of earth and stone, the stone being derived from weathered sandstone outcrops in the immediate vicinity (Fowke, 1902: 245). The earth fill in the walls was apparently taken from a ditch which averaged about 50 feet in width and was located along the inside edge of the wall (Morgan and Thomas, 1948: 31). A recent excavation of these walls indicates that they, like the walls of the Old Stone Fort, are composed of inclusive inner and outer walls of stone slabs filled and capped with earth and stone (personal communication with Raymond S. Baby, August 13, 1966).

It would be logical to use stone for building if it were readily available, so the use of stone in the Ohio enclosures does not prove that they are related to the Old Stone Fort. But similar methods of construction—such as horizontal slabs beneath the walls and inner and outer inclusive walls capped with earth and stone—may indicate a relationship between the Ohio enclosures and the Old Stone Fort; and the added features such as complex entranceways tend to confirm such a relationship.

There are no cul-de-sac entranceways as such in the Ohio hilltop enclosures, but several have gateways involving additional embankments of earth; these entrances might have had the same function. At Spruce Hill, the only level and easily accessible route into the enclosure was commanded by an entrance composed of three gateways. At each gateway, the ends of the outer wall were turned inward at right angles for a distance of 40 to 50 feet, with a passage between them about 8 feet wide (Squire and Davis, 1848: 11–12). Concerning these gateways Fowke later observed, "Thus, every entrance could be speedily closed to form a *cul-de-sac* where an enemy, when he once got in, would find himself exposed to attack on three sides" (1902: 242).

At "Fortified Hill," the main entrance at the north end was protected by an outer crescent embankment and four inner walls that form a kind of maze (Squire and Davis, 1848: 16–18). More noteworthy, however, are the gateways at the south and east sides of the enclosure. According to Squire and Davis, these entrances are "Tlascalan gateways": parallel walls of earth and stone constructed from the entrance into the interior of the enclosure. Both walls supposedly turn 90° before they end, forming what appears to be a narrower exit from the corridor (see Squire and Davis, 1848: Plate VI). However, Fowke states, "The so-called 'Tlascalan gateways' at the other end of the enclosure are so overgrown with trees and bushes, that it is impossible to ascertain whether they are correctly figured or not . . ." (1902: 259). If Squire and Davis are correct, these structures conform closely to the entrance complex of the Old Stone Fort.

Mounds of earth and stone figure prominently in the entrance complexes of some of these Ohio sites, and their occurrence is reminiscent of the two pedestal mounds that dominate the entrance of the Old Stone Fort. These mounds on the Ohio sites either are part of the wall or are detached and located somewhere in front of the main gateway. At Fort Ancient, both types of mounds are present. In the Great Gateway at the narrowest portion of the plateau, Squire and Davis noted and described two mounds (1848: 20). These are actually "the elevated terminations of the walls on the sides," according to a later description of this gateway (Moorehead, 1890: 81); and there is a possibility that inhumation was connected with these "mounds" since Moorehead states that "At their bases and between them is a raised platform four feet in height. This is more extensive on the side next to the Old Fort than on that lying toward the New, and when examined it was found to contain many human bones, in small fragments and much decayed" (p. 24).

Outside the East Gateway of the North Fort stand two mounds that were originally over ten feet in height (Moorehead, 1890: 51–52). Later descriptions of these tumuli suggest they were burial mounds (Morgan, 1946: 7), although Moorehead's excavation of these mounds indicated habitation debris in the fill but no conclusive evidence of inhumation. This led Moorehead to conclude that "The two mounds, supposed to be so rich in remains, were found to contain nothing. The first one may have been used as a burial tumulus, but no evidence of it now exists. If there were any skeletons deposited therein, they have long since been reduced to dust. If the two mounds were not intended for some purpose, ceremonial or observatory in character, we can assign no other use for them" (1890: 53).

At "Fortified Hill," a large mound ten feet in height was located outside the approach to the north gateway. Since an earlier excavation in the mound apparently produced no burials, Squire and Davis concluded that this was "used perhaps as an alarm post" (1848: 17). While it is entirely possible that both this mound and the structures at Fort Ancient were actually burial mounds, the suggestion that they were pedestals for "ceremony" or "observation" is more intriguing. In any case, their location, like that at the Old Stone Fort, suggests an important function in the entranceways.

A ditch in direct association with an entranceway is reported only at Fort Ancient, although possibly future excavation in the gateways of some of the other Ohio enclosures will reveal additional occurrences of this feature. At Fort Ancient a ditch was dug between each mound in front of the East Gateway and the edge of the ridge. These ditches were first noted by Caleb Atwater, who called them "gutters running nearly north and south, that appear to be artificial, and made to communicate with the branches on each side" (1820: 157). One of these ditches was tested by Moorehead who concluded that the ditch "is artificial, without doubt," although he admits, "We can assign no reason for this ditch, and its use is purely conjectural" (1890: 100).

The complex entranceways shared by some of the Ohio enclosures and the Old Stone Fort seem to be rare or absent on other enclosures in the Southeast. It is very probable that these different methods of construction in the Southeast are due to differences in function since some of the "enclosures" really enclose nothing and can be more justifiably called "stone constructions" (see Smith, 1962). Those that were built in isolated or inaccessible locales and/or seemed actually to be enclosures include Mount Carbon in Fayette County, West Virginia (Ingram, *et al.*, 1961; Kellar, 1961), Old Fort in Saline County, Missouri (Fowke, 1910: 82–86), a site at the confluence of the Town and South forks of the Elkhorn River near Lexington, Kentucky (Squire and Davis, 1848: 26); Indian Fort Mountain in Madison County, Kentucky (Young, 1910: 75–84; Funkhouser and Webb, 1932: 263); Fort Mountain near Chatsworth, Georgia (Moorehead, 1932: 155; Smith, 1962: 5–14); Alec Mountain in Habersham County, Georgia (Smith, 1962: 15); Sand Mountain in Catoosa County, Georgia (Smith, 1962: 16); Ladd Mountain near Cartersville, Georgia (Whittlesey, 1883: 677; Smith, 1962: 18); and De Soto Falls in northeastern Alabama (Roberts, 1949: 18–21; Smith, 1962: 28). It should be noted that this is not an exhaustive list of stone walls or enclosures in the Southeast, nor are the references cited the only ones pertaining to these sites. These sites were chosen because they *might* be temporally associated with the Old Stone Fort, and the reference listed for each one is the major source or the most recent treatise on the site.

Whether the purpose of these structures was defense has been seriously questioned, especially by more recent authors. This is particularly true of those walls which do not form an enclosure, such as the Mount Carbon and Sand Mountain walls. At the former site, windrows of stone seem to block access to the ridge, but these structures are not continuous and form a rather ineffective barrier (Kellar, 1961: 17). The wall at Sand Mountain was constructed between two cliffs, but one author concludes "it would in itself offer little resistance to attackers" (Smith, 1962: 17).

At some of these sites, it appears that an effort was made to block off the approaches to a high hill or ridge or to erect a barricade that would isolate the high point of a ridge. At Indian Fort Mountain a wall of stone was constructed across the neck of the ridge which leads to the top of the mountain, and additional walls were built at pregnable approaches to the summit (Young, 1910: 75–78). The stone wall at Fort Mountain is located near a narrow portion of the ridge which leads to the summit, but Smith emphasizes that the wall would have no strategic value for defenders since it meanders inconsistently across the ridge (1962: 8–9). At De Soto Falls two semicircular walls and a ditch enclose a portion of the ridge above the Little River (Roberts, 1949: 20).

Four of these sites have walls that form enclosures, although these embankments are broken by so-called "gateways" and in one instance by a stream. The Elkhorn River enclosure covered an area of about fifteen acres and was delimited by walls that were cut by a stream and by at least one entranceway (see Squire and Davis, 1848: Plate IX, No. 3). In Georgia, two enclosures are noteworthy, although one on Ladd Mountain in Bartow County was destroyed for road building material (Smith, 1962: 18). A 19th century sketch indicates that the walls were constructed in an oval pattern and were broken by six entrances (Whittlesey, 1883: 677). The walls on Alec Mountain form a broad oval; the north-south outside diameter is about 107 feet, but the east-west width is only about 92 feet (Smith, 1962: 15). The site was tested in the summer of 1956, but no cultural material was found (Smith, 1962: 15). At the Old Fort in Saline County, Missouri, an earth wall about 2,700 feet long encloses an area of more than six acres (Fowke, 1910: 85).

Although there are openings that may have been entrances in the walls of several of these sites, in only one instance are complex entrance walls evident—at the Old Fort in Missouri. Here overlapping parallel walls are found at the north end of the enclosure, and at least two short inner walls are located at the opposite end (Fowke, 1910: Figure 18). Concerning these entranceways, Fowke states: "The most accessible and vulnerable part is at the northern extremity; here the overlapping ends of the wall compel a detour in entering. At the opposite end, where there is a considerable level area outside the walls, protection is insured, or augmented, by a complicated arrangement of minor embankments and trenches" (1910: 83). Perhaps a similar feature is an inner embankment in the Elkhorn River site (Squire and Davis, 1848: Plate IX, No. 3). Only two other ditches seem to be present. Ditches seem to have been an integral part of the construction at the Old Fort in Missouri; Fowke relates that "the wall was built with earth taken up on both sides, leaving a continuous ditch within and a ditch or level strip without" (1910: 85). Although an earlier report indicates that these ditches were at least three feet deep (Broadhead, 1880: 356), a trench dug by Fowke across the embankment and ditches "showed the fill from wash and natural accumulation to be only a foot deep in the outer ditch or level area, and about 18 inches in the inner ditch; and some of this was due to plowing" (1910: 85). A shallow ditch is also present at De Soto Falls in front of the inner semicircular wall. This seems to have been dug to a depth of only one to two feet (Roberts, 1949: 19).

There are some similarities between Tennessee's Old Stone Fort and these other southeastern enclosures. It might be significant that most of the walls are low (not over four to five feet in height), and the placement of the structures in relatively inaccessible locations must also have significance. Another intriguing characteristic is that all of these sites except two have produced little or no cultural material, and only one had mounds within the enclosure. Cultural material was recovered within the walls at Mount Carbon, but this workshop debris could be from an earlier occupation (Kellar, 1961: 17). At Indian Fort Mountain it was reported that "in this locality has been found some of the few copper articles which have been discovered in Kentucky and certain of these objects were very evidently intended to serve as parts of a crude armor for the protection of the body" (Funkhouser and Webb, 1928: 78). If copper artifacts were actually found at this site, possibly the so-called "crude armor" was copper breastplates, artifacts typical of the Middle Woodland period.

Four mounds are reported within the Missouri Old Fort enclosure near the north entrance. Fowke states that when the mounds were previously opened "many skeletons were exhumed from a depth of 18 to 20 inches beneath the surface, 'piled in on one another as if all thrown in at one time' " (1910: 86). A relationship between these burials and the builders of the Missouri Old Fort has not been definitely established, but the similarity between this site and the Ohio hilltop enclosures is striking. Chapman concludes that "it may be significant that the only earthwork comparable to those found in Ohio Hopewell is found in Saline County, which seems to be the area of greatest concentration of Hopewellian village sites in [Missouri]" (1947: 83).

One other trait that might relate these sites and help identify their builders is the occurrence of stone mounds near these enclosures. Although common use of stone is not clear proof of a relationship between the mounds and the walls, their repeated joint occurrence suggests that they were built at about the same time. This association has been noted not only in the Southeast but also in Ohio (for instance, at Fort Ancient, where some of the burials found under stone piles have been tentatively identified [Kellar, 1960: 432] as late Middle Woodland).

In the Southeast, stone mounds or cairns have been found in or near several enclosures or walls. At Mount Carbon, several stone piles inside the walled area were investigated, but no definite conclusions could be drawn since of those tested some were of recent construction and others seemed to be natural occurrences of stone (Kellar, 1961: 15–16). Six stone cairns are located on Sand Mountain, but in a recent investigation of one, no remains were discovered (Smith, 1962: 17). In Georgia, stone mounds are said to be found in almost every northern county and are commonly located in upland areas (Kellar, 1960: 456). One of these tumuli was the Shaw Mound, located near the Ladd Mountain enclosure. When the rock in this mound was removed for road material, a burial was discovered. Associated with this inhumation were several large sheets of mica, a trapezoidal copper breastplate, two greenstone celts, a copper celt, and fragments of what might have been a cut-design copper ornament (Waring, 1945: 119). The

Hopewell and Copena-like cast of these artifacts led Waring to conclude: "Thus, it seems most likely, in the light of direct evidence from the Shaw Mound and of indirect evidence from comparable sites, that there existed in Georgia a complex probably contemporaneous with Hopewell in Ohio, 'Copena' in Alabama, and Marksville in Louisiana" (p. 120).

Although separate stone or earth tumuli are not directly associated with Tennessee's Old Stone Fort, numerous small mounds are scattered through Middle Tennessee. There is a possibility that some occur in the vicinity of the Old Stone Fort, since Jones states that "In the woods northwest of the fort, several piles of rock were observed, about two feet high and ten feet in diameter. When these were removed, they were found to have covered a layer of ashes, charcoal, and burned earth. They are supposed to have marked the place of the incineration of human bodies. These were the only remains resembling graves which were discovered" (1876: 103).

Although the presence of these cairns was not verified during the 1966 field season, some attempt was made to locate habitation sites in the vicinity of the Old Stone Fort that might have been occupied by the builders of this enclosure. Woodland pottery had been reported in rock shelters near the site, but no ceramic-producing site was discovered by the 1966 reconnaissance party. This was somewhat surprising, since Jones states that he found "fragments of pottery" along the Duck River (p. 103), and other early writers indicate that pottery-producing sites are located in the area.

These reports indicate that Woodland peoples were undoubtedly in the area, and an artifact figured by Jones also suggests that some of these people had affinities or contact with a Copena group. A bird effigy pipe carved from steatite (see Plate 6) was supposedly found "near the Stone Fort and Cave in the vicinity of Manchester, Tennessee" (Jones, 1876: Figure 58). It is now in the collection of the Museum of the American Indian, Heye Foundation, in New York City. The only statement about its origin is that it was excavated prior to 1875 near Manchester in Coffee County. This pipe appears to be in the same style as the dog effigy pipe found in a Copena mound in Lawrence County, Alabama (Webb, 1939: 47–

Plate 6: Effigy pipe in the Museum of the American Indian, Heye Foundation. Found near the Old Stone Fort. (Photograph courtesy of Museum of the American Indian, Heye Foundation.)

51) and the five steatite effigy pipes from Seip Mound No. 1 in Ross County, Ohio (Shetrone and Greenman, 1931: 416–24).

An apparent lack of Woodland remains in the area immediately around the Old Stone Fort should not be construed as an additional enigma of this site. A more intensive survey of the area will probably reveal Woodland sites, either buried by river silt or hidden in uncultivated areas. But even if these sites are not close to the Old Stone Fort, there is a logical explanation of where the builders of this enclosure lived. This scarcity of large habitation sites around ceremonial centers is also characteristic of some Ohio Hopewell sites, and the phenomenon has led Prufer to conclude "that it reflects a settlement pattern similar to the classic Mesoamerican situation of the vacant ceremonial centers—semi-permanent shifting agricultural village type. In other words, what we are facing here seem to be elaborate ceremonial centers based upon a mortuary cult and surrounded by very small dependent villages of little permanence" (1964: 71). If such a situation existed in Middle Tennessee during Middle Woodland times, people from a widespread area could have assembled periodically to build and maintain the Old Stone Fort.

When one searches further for evidence of Middle Woodland occupation in this area, it becomes apparent that an attenuated burial mound complex existed in Middle Tennessee related to Copena and Ohio Hopewell. Several mounds have been reported in the Nashville area, including a large stone mound on Reid Hill in Williamson County that Jennings (1946: 126) equates with the Shaw mound. Unfortunately, no diagnostic material from Reid Hill is known to exist. A copper earspool was found in Williamson County, "deeply imbedded in a large mound, in a layer of ashes and burned clay . . ." (Thurston, 1890: 302). Possibly this artifact was in the Reid Hill mound or in one of two smaller mounds about a mile west of the former tumulus that Jennings described as having "been pitted in the past" (1946: 126). Putnam (1882: 166–67, 110–11, 121–22) also describes material from a large mound near Franklin in Williamson County. An excavation by E. C. Curtis for the Peabody Museum in 1879 produced copper artifacts such as earspools, an axe, and a conjoined tube, plus some galena and red ocher.

Early excavation of a mound five miles east of Lebanon, Tennessee, produced "two thin copper plates, about eleven inches long, four inches wide, and about a tenth of an inch thick" (Thruston, 1897: 302). If these were copper breastplates, they are very typical of Ohio Hopewell. The most striking copper artifact with Hopewell-Copena affinities, however, is a reel-shaped gorget found with a platform pipe in a mound in Marshall County, Tennessee (Thurston, 1897: 352j; Plate XV, A). The Duck River flows through the northern portion of Marshall County, which is about forty miles west of Coffee County.

Reel-shaped copper gorgets are very characteristic of the Copena remains found on the Tennessee River in northern Alabama. Webb states that "So far as the author is aware there have been only two copper reel-shaped objects reported from the southeastern United States outside the immediate vicinity of the Tennessee River" (1939: 193). Significantly these artifacts have also been recovered in Ohio Hopewell sites, notably at Tremper Mound (Mills, 1916: 210–15) and from the Hopewell village site at Fort Ancient (Mills, 1916: 213; Morgan, 1946: 39).

Other artifacts found in mounds in Middle Tennessee are common in the Copena burial complex. These include earspools, copper breastplates, and galena. Although the evidence is scanty, it appears that a Copena-like complex was present in this area during Middle Woodland times.

Copena has been recently dubbed "Alabama Hopewell," but this popular use of the term Hopewell should not lead to the incorrect conclusion that the two groups were identical. Although it now appears that Copena and Ohio Hopewell were contemporaneous for at least part of their existence, they seem to have been related largely because of their participation in a pan-regional trade network involving mortuary paraphernalia. A pan-regional Hopewell "culture" does not seem to have existed, nor are these even regional expressions of one Middle Woodland culture (Struever, 1965). Thus to name the Hopewell culture as builders of the mounds and the Old Stone Fort in Middle Tennessee would probably be imprudent.

Although the similarities between Copena and this local Middle Woodland culture appear to be quite strong, it would also be presumptuous to state that Copena people were responsible for the Old Stone Fort. The Copena "culture" is still imperfectly known except for a burial complex, and at the present time Copena can be considered only as a regional mortuary complex in the Middle Woodland period. This regional complex appears to be centered in northern Alabama along the Tennessee River and its tributaries. Although there are many parallels with the mortuary complex of Ohio Hopewell, particularly in artifact types, enclosures do not seem to be a part of the Copena trait complex. Enclosures might be more typical of the group that built some of the earthworks at the Pinson Mounds site on the Forked Deer River in Madison

County, Tennessee, a group tentatively identified as late Middle Woodland or Marksville (Fischer and McNutt, 1962: 11; Morse and Polhemus, n.d.). It might be significant that a circular structure is located outside one of the gateways in the embankment at the Marksville site (Fowke, 1928: 412–13). Since at the present time the earth and stone embankment is the only trait that seems to relate Pinson Mounds to the Old Stone Fort, any suggestion of Marksville influences is certainly premature.

Since we know so little about Middle Woodland in Middle and West Tennessee, our conclusions about this period are academic. It does appear, however, that there were at least three related groups of people inhabiting this portion of Tennessee and northern Alabama: one group with a regional mortuary complex we call Copena in northern Alabama; one with Marksville characteristics in West Tennessee, with a center at Pinson; and a group in Middle Tennessee that built stone mounds and the enclosure known as the Old Stone Fort. The artifacts associated with this last group suggest close affinities with Alabama Copena and also ties to Ohio Hopewell. All seem to have partaken in the pan-regional trade network and shared the distinctive mortuary customs that were so typical of Middle Woodland times.

AGE OF THE OLD STONE FORT

THE PRE-COLUMBIAN AGE of the fort has been known since Haywood's discourse when he revealed that a tree growing in the wall which had been cut down in 1819 had 357 rings (1823: 160). In an attempt to discover exactly when this structure was built, the 1966 investigators collected 17 charcoal samples from the walls for radiocarbon dating. Of the 17 samples collected, 13 were eventually rejected because of possible contamination or insufficient quantity. Only one sample plausibly dated an *in situ* association with a constructional feature. The other acceptable samples were from either charcoal scatter or pockets that presumably had been included in the embankment fill. Unless the burning happened when the wall was built, this charcoal could give only a maximum date for the Old Stone Fort. Four samples were submitted to Geochron Laboratories, Inc., Cambridge, Massachusetts, for dating. One *in situ* sample was from the entrance ditch, and the other three were from charcoal deposits in the entrance complex and outer walls. On November 3, 1966, the following results were received from Geochron Laboratories (Faulkner, 1967: 19–20):

TABLE 1: RESULTS OF RADIOCARBON DATING OF CHARCOAL SAMPLES

Sample Number	Date & *Age*	Composition	Source
GXO773	A.D. 305 *1645 ± 90 years B.P.*	Wood charcoal apparently included with a load of white and reddish clay.	Trench 2, in the south wall, at a depth of 4-4.5 feet.
GXO774	A.D. 220 *1730 ± 90 years B.P.*	Wood charcoal.	Small pocket in east profile of Trench 5, just above rubble floor in south wall, at depth of 4.1 feet.
GXO775	A.D. 430 *1520 ± 95 years B.P.*	Wood charcoal mixed with clay and rock.	Trench 10, at the north terminus of west entrance wall, 2.3 feet from surface.
GXO776	A.D. 30 *1920 ± 85 years B.P.*	Wood charcoal.	Feature 4, entrance ditch. Sample was associated with fired area at bottom, 4.3 feet from surface.

At first glance, the above dates do not seem to be consistent among themselves, which might initially cast some doubt on their validity. However, when one remembers that the enclosure obviously was not built in a short time and that there is evidence of a sequence of constructional features, the dates become more congruent. Also, there is the possibility that the first three dates tell only the age of the charcoal itself, not when the walls were actually erected. However, it might not be coincidence that the first two dates—from the outer walls—are within 85 years of one another. Considering probable error, the deposits in the south wall possibly date in the late 3rd century A.D.

If the radiocarbon dates are correct for the constructional stages of this enclosure, they are entirely consistent with the archaeological findings. There is evidence that the entrance ditch is earlier than the parallel entrance walls, since the latter overlap a stacked stone retainer-fill in the ditch. Since the charcoal constituting Sample GXO776 was associated with burned earth at the bottom of the ditch, it is reasonable to assume this fire occurred while the ditch was open and in use sometime during the 1st century A.D. Although not enough dates are available to prove that the ditch was dug across the narrow access route at the same time the outer walls of the enclosure were raised, the gap between the date for the ditch and the charcoal in the south wall indicates the latter was not completed until the 3rd century A.D. Significantly, the latest date is from the parallel walls of the cul-de-sac, which logically might be expected to be a later addition. If the date for the entrance wall truly marks the completion of this structure, a span of four hundred years for its erection can be posited. It may seem incredible that building a structure for defense would take this long; accretive construction might be more in keeping with a ceremonial function. These possible functions will be discussed in the following section.

Falling within the initial centuries of the Christian Era, these dates allow us to place the building of the Old Stone Fort within a definite period of Southeastern prehistory—the Middle Woodland period. Although this period in Tennessee is still imperfectly known, in the Ohio Valley it is characterized by the emergence and demise of the Hopewell culture. The Hopewell culture is now generally believed to date approximately between 400 B.C. and A.D. 400.[7] Some writers such as Prufer (1964) believe that most of the Ohio hilltop enclosures were built during the waning years of the Hopewell culture. A recently determined date from an Ohio

[7]Radiocarbon dates obtained in the early 1950's suggested that the distinctive Hopewell culture might have been in existence as early as 400 B.C. (Griffin, 1958: 1). However, numerous radiocarbon samples tested since 1959 all seem to post-date 100 B.C. (personal communication with Stuart Struever, June 30, 1967).

enclosure not only strengthens this theory, but also correlates well with the later dates obtained from the Old Stone Fort. Charcoal associated with an early construction phase at Fort Miami in Hamilton County, Ohio, has been dated at 1680 ± 130 years ago (A.D. 270).[8] Although the data is still scanty, it seems that the Old Stone Fort and at least some of the Ohio hilltop enclosures were built around the same time.

FUNCTION OF THE OLD STONE FORT

CERTAINLY the most vexing question about the Old Stone Fort concerns the nature of its function. The puzzle may never be solved unless additional field work is undertaken here and at other, similar enclosure sites in the eastern United States.

According to some local and even professional interpretations, the problem has already been solved—the structure was used for defense. The name popularly given to this enclosure suggests itself that specific function. Even the author found himself using such descriptive terms for features of its construction as "vulnerable," "defensive," and "battlements," although a serious attempt was made to consistently refer to the structure as an enclosure. All of this indicates a general tendency to consider the structure a "fort," built for defensive purposes. Concomitant with this line of reasoning is the idea that all enclosures or even stone constructions had the same martial function.

This faulty reasoning not only disregards the fact that some of these phenomena could not possibly serve as defensive works but also ignores the vagaries of human behavior. Our own ethnocentric thinking leads us to equate the large amount of labor connected with these sites and the raising of substantial walls with some exigency, such as defense. In actuality, however, the builders' motives might have been entirely different from ours.

No attempt will be made here to synthesize the data on stone constructions or stone and earth embankments in general. Since

[8]University of Michigan Radiocarbon Laboratories Sample No. M-1869. This date is published with the kind permission of James B. Griffin, University of Michigan, and Fred W. Fischer, University of Cincinnati.

the Old Stone Fort falls into a class of these phenomena called "enclosures," any theories about the Tennessee site could refer to other constructions and vice versa. Although the author would like to be imaginative, the paucity of data on these sites engenders caution. This limits the discussion of the Old Stone Fort's function to two rather broad theories which have been promulgated for years: the "defensive" and the "ceremonial" theories. It is hoped that 1966 data from the Old Stone Fort will aid in examining these theories.

The earliest writers to wrestle with the function of the enclosures were quite emphatic about their being true forts. Squire and Davis (1848: 9) concluded:

> The natural strength of such positions, and their susceptibility of defence, would certainly suggest them as the citadels of a people having hostile neighbors, or pressed by invaders. Accordingly we are not surprised at finding these heights occupied by strong and complicated works, the design of which is no less indicated by their position than by their construction. But in such cases, it is always to be observed, that they have been chosen with great care, and that they possess peculiar strength, and have a special adaptation for the purposes to which they were applied. They occupy the highest points of land, and are never commanded from neighboring positions. While rugged and steep on most sides, they have one or more points of comparatively easy approach, in the protection of which the utmost skill of the builders seems to have been exhausted. They are guarded by double, overlapping walls, or a series of them, having sometimes an accompanying mound, designed perhaps for a look-out, and corresponding to the barbican in the system of defence of the Britons of the middle era. The usual defence is a simple embankment, thrown up along and a little below the brow of the hill, varying in height and solidity, as the declivity is more or less steep and difficult of access.

This viewpoint remained virtually unchallenged in the first decades of the 20th century. Fowke concluded that "the method of construction and their position relative to the surrounding country, make it obvious they were intended as a place of refuge in time of danger from foes" (1902: 238); and Shetrone echoes these popular sentiments by later stating they were "obviously intended for purposes of defense" (1930: 223).

Although later writers such as Morgan (1946 and 1952) have questioned the idea that the structures were exclusively used as defensive "forts," a current worker in the Ohio Valley still champions the long-standing defensive theory. Olaf Prufer has presented data that suggest the hilltop enclosures of Ohio were constructed near the end of the Hopewell occupation in Ohio when the population was forced to take defensive measures against some major threat (1964: 69–70).

If the Ohio hilltop enclosures were indeed forts, their similarity to the Tennessee site suggests that it, too, was defensive in nature. Certainly the pedestals (lookout platforms?), ditch, cul-de-sac entranceway, and walls placed only where easy penetration was possible are typical components of fortifications, especially when found together. When each is considered independently, however, certain inconsistencies arise.

One inconsistency is the apparent long period of time it took to build the enclosure. A possible explanation for an extended period of building activity is that attack was not always imminent, and when there was no threat, the builders had time to improve their position. Another inconsistency is the rather ineffective nature of some of the walls after they were built, particularly if no additional barricade surmounted them. The walls obviously would have been ineffective because they lack height and because they encompass an extensive area. The walls' height might have been increased by erecting a palisade atop the earth and stone embankment, but no evidence of such a feature was discovered in the excavations.

Even if the enclosure were palisaded, since the area was so large, a sizable force of defenders would have been necessary to man the walls. The idea that such large numbers of Indians were involved might be questioned, since Driver maintains that "fights between whole tribes seem to have been rare before White contact" (1961: 370); and Turney-High states that "The typical American Indian war party . . . was a force too small . . . to make the principle of cooperation of much significance" (1949: 55). There is, however, a definite possibility that inter-tribal warfare did occur occasionally in the East during prehistoric times. One of these occasions might have been the legendary war between the prehistoric Lenni Lenape and the Tallegewi or Alligewi (Lilly *et al.*, 1954: 134–35), if indeed this war took place. The mass grave at Fort Ancient and the possible evidence of conflagration at some of the hilltop enclosures have been cited by Prufer as evidence for such a large-scale war (1964: 69).

Another incongruous element is the virtual absence of occupational debris inside the Old Stone Fort and similar enclosures. If the enclosures were built to be occupied in time of danger, some of them were apparently never needed. The only interpretation here seems to be that these were citadels which were maintained for a long duration because of an ever-present threat. This might have been similar to the Inca settlement pattern where "Towns were never fortified, the inhabitants maintaining instead a fort or 'city of refuge' on some peak near the peacetime settlement" (Rowe, 1946: 228).

Because of the unresolved questions about the defense of such large enclosures and the lack of occupational debris in many of them, recent writers have sought another explanation for the structures. The vogue now is to explain them as "ceremonial," a term that begs the question since "ceremonial" can cover a wide range of human behavior. The term can be used to imply that religious activities took place in these structures; however, the goal of the archaeologist is to recover enough data to make specific inferences about these activities. Sears states in a recent article that "Data on the ceremonial activities, and the religious and political systems of these prehistoric cultures is most likely to have been 'fossilized' in structures built for, during, or as a by-product of, major ceremonies" (1961: 227); but a dearth of remains from human activity of any kind in the enclosures certainly restricts the possibility of more specific inferences. Of course it is entirely possible that the *lack* of cognitive remains in the Old Stone Fort may be the most meaningful "fossilized" evidence at this site.

Morgan became one of the earliest exponents of the "ceremonial school" of thought when he wrote: "It now seems evident that the

Fort Ancient Earthworks were not built solely for defensive purposes as some previous writers have claimed, but that the 'Fort'
proper, like the geometrical enclosures of the lowlands, was also
used for ceremonial rites" (1946: 13–15). Later he continues to
support the theory that they were ceremonial centers and cites
evidence that "Burial mounds were built within and adjacent to
the hill-top enclosures in a few cases, and they have features such
as parallel walls, paved ways and burial mounds which seem to
have had ceremonial functions. Although the hill-top enclosures
have been termed 'forts,' it is evident that they were used as ceremonial centers as well as for defense" (1952: 89).

Other writers are also of the opinion that the enclosures were
ceremonial in nature. Carl Chapman has concluded: "The enclosures on hill-tops in southwestern and north central Missouri were
probably constructed for ceremonial purposes. These may be large
and have mounds associated with them. The Hopewell culture was
probably responsible for their construction. A good example of this
type is the 'Old Fort' in the Van Meter State Park, Saline County,
Missouri" (1953: 17).

While some of the Ohio hilltop enclosures may be involved in
the Hopewell mortuary complex, there is nothing in Tennessee's
Old Stone Fort to suggest that it functioned in mortuary rites.
Nevertheless, if the walls and the entranceway are interpreted as
having a sacred rather than a secular function, numerous possibilities arise. The walls cease to be barricades to prevent the incursion
of enemies, but become markers to enclose the sacred area. They
could have been a "no trespassing" symbol to the uninvited or un-
initiated. The entrance complex becomes a device that not only
deters intrusion during solemn ceremonies, but also provides an os-
tentatious setting for a spectacular entrance ceremony.

Although it is evident that a large force of laborers built the
structure and presumably used it at least periodically, thus far it
seems they left few prosaic articles within the walls. It is almost as
though an effort was made not to profane this sacred place with
mundane things. Raymond S. Baby shares this opinion when he
states that some sites "such as Fort Hill, were infrequently used,
[and] the small amount of midden, if any, resulting from use was

carefully and deliberately removed" (letter to author, December 12, 1966).

It is a well-established fact that many historic tribes in the eastern United States kept their town squares and ceremonial areas meticulously clean. Witthoft even reports that one feature present in the Creek Busk ceremony was "ritual disposal of earth removed from the square ground" (1949: 68). That the removal of earth from plaza areas was also practiced in prehistoric times is suggested by Ford's observation of the plaza at Greenhouse, a Troyville-Coles Creek period site: "The center of the area was remarkably free from refuse. It is possible that this was intentional and that the plaza was a bare, clay-surfaced courtyard that was regularly cleaned" (1951: 102). Recent excavation of the Whorley Earthwork in Branch County, Michigan (Speth, 1966), also revealed an enclosure that evidently was periodically swept clean. This evidence plus large gaps between the posts in an accompanying palisade that had an open end led Speth to conclude that the Michigan enclosure probably had a ceremonial function (1966: 220).

Besides mortuary ceremonialism, widespread trade relationships constitute another outstanding characteristic of the Ohio Hopewell culture. Since some ritual was obviously involved in the trade for ceremonial objects, the Old Stone Fort and other enclosures like it in the Southeast might have functioned in the intensive trade network that existed between the Gulf Coast and the Ohio Valley.[9] Possibly they were links in the trade routes back to the Hopewell centers. However, one would expect them to be on clearly defined routes if they functioned in this manner. Since the Old Stone Fort is not on a major north-south river, it does not seem to be in a meaningful position for water travel. Nevertheless, it is quite interesting that this enclosure was near a main north-south trail leading from Florida and Alabama on Franquelin's 1684 map of La Salle's discoveries. Myer (1928: 847) states:

> The trail shown on Franquelin's map is undoubtedly the trail leading from [the] Old Stone Fort, via Battle Creek and the Old Creek Crossing on the Tennessee River near Bridgeport, Ala., into

[9]The author would like to thank Stuart Struever for this most intriguing suggestion.

Georgia. . . . At the crossing it connected with a great network of trails which united many parts of Georgia and Alabama with the populous and numerous Cherokee towns in east Tennessee, and then continued in a southeast direction through Georgia to Augusta and from there to St. Augustine, Fla. . . .

Although it is not known whether this trail was in use during Middle Woodland times or that it had any relationship to the function of the Old Stone Fort, a connection cannot be entirely ruled out.

As noted earlier, radiocarbon dates suggest that the Old Stone Fort was constructed over a period of time. This refurbishing might indicate a strengthening of the installation for better protection. Usually, however, a defensive structure is built as quickly as possible, to meet some ominous threat. But if the structure was ceremonial in nature, it is likely that the walls were renovated as the rites became more important during several centuries of use.

The most baffling of all questions about the possible ceremonial nature of these enclosures is, exactly what ceremonies took place in the inner sanctum sanctorum? Whether the enclosure was erected to protect a scattered populace from the wrath of enemies or to aid them in making peace with their gods, a great amount of toil was required to complete and maintain it. Such great effort is testimony for the importance of the enclosure to its builders. As the state of Tennessee prepares to restore this site to its original configuration, more fieldwork should be undertaken, both to aid in the correct restoration of the site and to provide the needed data on why it was built. If we can discover what actually motivated prehistoric people to construct the "Old Stone Fort," we will have taken an important step in determining what social and religious systems were operative in Tennessee and the Southeast during Middle Woodland times.

Descriptive Report and Excavations at the Old Stone Fort

The Outer Walls: Early Accounts

WILLIAM DONNISON's eyewitness account of the Old Stone Fort embankments is one of the earliest (1819) of the more cogent de-

Plate 7: The south wall of the Old Stone Fort. At this point the wall was built well below the crest of the natural plateau which can be seen to the right of the photograph.

scriptions and appears to have been a source for later writers. Donnison observed that the walls terminated at the steep cliffs on the east and west sides of the ridge, and that the material used was stone. His dimensions of the walls might be somewhat exaggerated, but this should be expected if his measurements were mere speculations. The heights of only two walls were noted: the north wall, "about 10 feet perpendicular" on the inner face, and "the south wall, on its inner side, about 8 feet in height." An entrance or gateway in this south wall is mentioned. The only other dimensions concern the width of the walls, which are "generally of the same thickness, being about 16 or 20 feet at the base, and on top from 4 to 5 feet through."

Haywood's discourse (1823: 158–59) so closely follows the above that to present it here would be superfluous. However, it does contain a statement by Col. Andrew Erwin, who owned the Old Stone Fort property in 1819, that "The wall . . . is mouldered down so as to be at present about 16 feet wide on the surface of the earth, about six feet high" (p. 160).

Apparently the next independent and therefore pertinent statement concerning the Old Stone Fort is contained in a letter by T. C. Yoakim, dated January 25, 1845, from Murfreesboro, Tennessee. Yoakim obviously visited the site and had this to say about the walls: "The parapet is now, in some places five or six feet high, and was originally perhaps ten feet high. The ditch being inside the Fort. There is not the least evidence of any iron tool having been used about it. The wall is of dirt—and, about the entrance loose pebbles and flint rock." Here, the two noteworthy features not mentioned in previous reports are the presence of earth in the wall fill and the existence of an interior ditch. No entrance in the south wall is mentioned.

In 1876 Joseph Jones reconnoitered the enclosure and the area around it. He concurs with the earlier writers that the walls are mainly composed of rock carried from the stream banks, although he also mentions that "in some portions of the wall, earth has been freely mixed with them" (1876: 101). This antiquarian also states that the wall was from four to ten feet in height and mentions a ditch on the inside of the front or north wall. His map (see Plate 2) and verbal account do not indicate a south gateway (1876: 100–101).

Cox's Excavations in the Outer Walls

During two weeks in early September, 1928, P. E. Cox and four workmen excavated five trenches through the walls of the enclosure. Four of these trenches were cut into the outer wall; the other was cut in the west wall of the entranceway (see Figure 2). Trench 1 was in the east wall, approximately 215 feet from the entrance. The second trench was in the southeast corner of the south wall. Trench 3 was placed in the center of the south wall; and Trench 4, in the west wall of the entranceway. Trench 5 was dug in the west wall about 200 feet from the entrance. These cuts through the outer walls are indicated by a "C" and the corresponding trench number on Figure 2. The results of these tests are summarized below.

In 1928 the average height of the walls was five feet, although the tested portion of the west wall was only four feet high. The average thickness of the base of the embankment varied from 16 to 18 feet, the variation being explained by erosion. Cox (1929: 2–4) concluded that the entire structure was built from chunks and slabs of rock, all of it obtained from naturally weathered bedrock in the local stream beds. Although the excavator makes the general statement that "The walls are constructed entirely of fragments of flint and slabs of shale heaped together" (p. 2), he does indicate that there were different proportions of shale and "flint" in the fill, and that part of the base of the east wall consisted of a layer of river gravel. Another phenomenon reported by Cox was a "hearth" or "firebox," discovered near the base of the wall in Trenches 1 and 3.

1966 Excavations in the Outer Walls

Seven trenches were cut through the outer walls (see Figure 2). *Trench 1*—This trench was 5 feet wide by 30 feet long, excavated 978.7 feet from the benchmark at the east end of the south wall. This measurement is to the west profile of the trench. A 5 by 5 foot extension was added to test the inner edge of the wall. The wall at this point was 4.45 feet high at the crest. The method of construction was generally the same as that of the other walls, but with several variations. Inner and outer walls of chert rubble, shale slabs, and limestone rock were built on a pavement of chert rock and slabs that extended between the two walls. The fill between the walls was a brown soil that also capped the entire embankment (see Figure 3 and Plate 8). The inner and outer walls were different: the inside wall was larger, with a core of shale slabs and chert rubble on the periphery (Plate 9), whereas the outer wall was smaller and had an almost vertical inner face of stacked slabs (Plate 10). To hold this vertical construction the builders must have piled earth against the stacked rock.

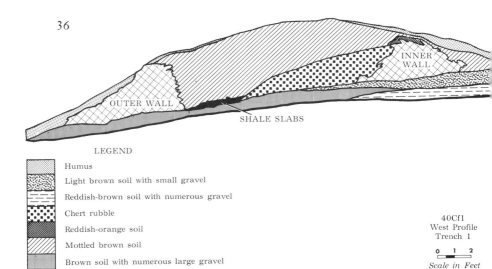

INNER WALL

OUTER WALL

SHALE SLABS

LEGEND

Humus

Light brown soil with small gravel

Reddish-brown soil with numerous gravel

Chert rubble

Reddish-orange soil

Mottled brown soil

Brown soil with numerous large gravel

40Cf1
West Profile
Trench 1

0   1   2
Scale in Feet

Figure 3: Trench 1, West Profile

Trench 2—The second trench dug through the south wall was also 5 feet wide by 30 feet long with a 5 by 5 foot extension. The west profile of this trench was 855 feet from the east end of the south wall or 123.7 feet east of Trench 1. The wall here was 4.5 feet in height and the construction was virtually identical to that revealed in Trench 1 (Plate 11). The inner and outer walls were composed of shale slabs and chert chunks, although not as much chert was present as in Trench 1. The earth fill between the two walls rested on scattered slabs placed on the old ground surface.

Trench 3—This trench was excavated at the eastern end of the south wall; its west profile was 59.4 feet from the benchmark and 795.6 feet east of Trench 2. The 3 feet wide by 30 feet long trench exposed a wall built almost entirely of stone with a capping of light yellow soil and gravel that reached a maximum height of 4.9 feet above the former ground level. The rock fill, which was about 95 per cent chert slabs in the center of the wall, was stacked in the middle with two lesser "peaks" that might have corresponded to inner and outer walls (Figure 4).

Trench 4—Another test excavation in the south wall was a 3 feet wide by 33 feet long trench with profiles that showed a poorly defined inner wall with a base composed of slabs. The west profile of

Plate 8: Trench 1—Shows the construction of the south wall. The outer inclusive wall can be seen in the profile in the upper left and the inner inclusive wall can be seen in the lower right. Chert rubble is between these two inclusive walls below the clay fill.

Plate 9: Trench 1—A close-up of the larger inner wall with a core of shale slabs and chert rubble on the periphery.

Plate 10: Trench 1—Slabs of the smaller outer inclusive wall as seen in the west profile of Trench 1. Note the almost vertical inner face of the stacked slabs.

Plate 11: Trench 2—The inner inclusive wall can be seen in the foreground and the outer inclusive wall is in the background. The scattered slabs on the original surface can be seen between these two inclusive walls.

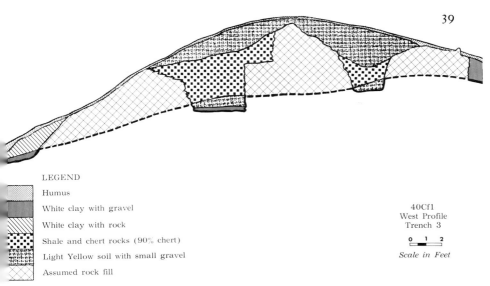

LEGEND

Humus

White clay with gravel

White clay with rock

Shale and chert rocks (90% chert)

Light Yellow soil with small gravel

Assumed rock fill

40Cf1
West Profile
Trench 3

0   1   2

Scale in Feet

Figure 4: Trench 3, West Profile

this unit was 258.1 feet west of the comparable profile of Trench 1. The outer wall was of chert rubble capped with shale slabs and cherty limestone boulders. An earth and rock fill was between the two inclusive walls. The top of the embankment at this point was 5.75 feet from the old ground surface.

Trench 5—This was an excavation perpendicular to the east profile of Trench 1. An original 5 by 20 foot trench was expanded into a 10 by 40 foot unit to expose the inner wall of the embankment.

Trench 6—A 3 feet wide by 29 feet long trench was dug through the east wall where the embankment was 3.6 feet high. The north profile of this trench was 681.8 feet from the entrance and 412.9 feet from the end of the wall at the east bluffs. Only a 3 by 10.5 foot area was excavated to the original ground surface; the remainder of the trench was dug 0.2 feet deep to expose the rock fill under the humus layer. The embankment here was constructed entirely of rock with much shale in the fill.

Trench 15—This 3 feet wide by 34 feet long trench was cut through the west wall, its north profile being 413.3 feet from the entrance. Two inclusive walls were readily apparent, and some

40

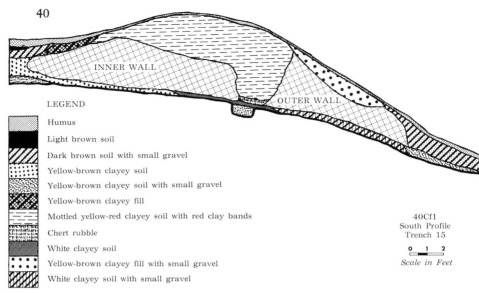

LEGEND

	Humus
	Light brown soil
	Dark brown soil with small gravel
	Yellow-brown clayey soil
	Yellow-brown clayey soil with small gravel
	Yellow-brown clayey fill
	Mottled yellow-red clayey soil with red clay bands
	Chert rubble
	White clayey soil
	Yellow-brown clayey fill with small gravel
	White clayey soil with small gravel

40Cf1
South Profile
Trench 15

0   1   2
Scale in Feet

Figure 5: Trench 15, South Profile

stacking was present on the inner face of the outer wall. Both walls were constructed primarily of cherty limestone blocks that sometimes weighed as much as seventy pounds. The fill between the inner and outer walls was earth and small rock, with lenses of red clay evident in the south profile (Figure 5). This was one of the rare examples of earth loading. The crest of the embankment here was 6.1 feet above the original ground surface (see Plate 12).

Conclusions about the Outer Walls

Although early descriptions do not agree on the height of the outer walls, those that indicate a range of four to six feet are probably the most nearly accurate. There is evidence that Donnison's 1819 estimate of eight feet for the south wall is an exaggeration: the profiles in the test trenches beyond the actual embankment do not show any extensive deposit from erosion, and there is no evidence that fill was removed from the east, west, or south walls. Thus, these three walls probably are about the same height as when they were initially raised. The statements that the north or front wall was ten feet high cannot be verified because it has been de-

Plate 12: The exterior face of the west wall of the Old Stone Fort. Trench 15 was cut through the wall near this point. The steep slope above the Duck River can be seen to the right.

stroyed by prior removal and road building. Since this wall faced a vulnerable approach, the suggestion that it was an imposing structure seems plausible.

Another point of disagreement among early observers is the presence of an interior ditch along the walls. Yoakim (1845) mentions a "ditch being inside the Fort," and Jones (1876) indicates that a ditch was present on the inner side of the front or north wall. This questionable feature was probably the slight depression of filled Feature 4 (see below). The test trenches dug through various portions of the outer walls did not reveal the presence of any other interior ditches.

The fact that rock composes most of the enclosure fill has been known since earliest recorded visits to the fort, and Cox's excavation helped establish this. Cox noted that the rock fill was not the same in all portions of the wall, but he failed to discover or report the most salient construction feature. This feature is a recurring theme of construction: inner and outer inclusive walls of shale slabs and chert boulders with a "cap" of mixed earth and rock. This theme recurs several times in the walls, with minor variations. Besides these variations, other methods of construction were also revealed by the 1966 excavations. At least one portion of the east wall was composed almost entirely of stone, and the southeastern end of the south wall appeared to have three separate inclusive "walls." Another type of construction occasionally used was stacked rock.

Since the walls were built at those places on the ridge that lacked the natural protection of the bluffs, it is possible that they were built for defensive purposes. However, two factors cast doubt on this interpretation: the walls are rather low to be an effective barrier, and no evidence of palisade posts was found in the fill. Although organic material would have disappeared rapidly in the clay soil of the area, it seems likely that rotting posts would have left some molds as evidence.

A definite scarcity of cultural material in the wall fill was noted in the 1966 excavation. Besides scattered charcoal and a few random chert flakes and chunks, no artifacts were found deep in the walls. Seven identifiable projectile points were recovered, but all except one were discovered near the edge of the embankment (see Table 2 and Plate 13) and could not be definitely associated with the erection of the wall. This paucity of cultural material is surprising in light of Cox's discovery of two "hearths" in the walls. Not only did Cox report finding these slab-lined fireplaces, filled with ashes, but he also stated he found charred bird, animal, and human bones plus two pieces of burned corn cob in the ash (1929: 4). Only two explanations are possible: either Cox was extremely fortunate to find these remains, or he misinterpreted what he saw. The latter explanation is plausible because a fine clay found in the wall fill superficially resembles white ash. However, even if Cox

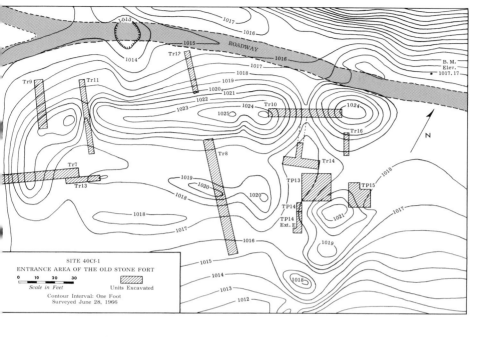

Figure 6: The Old Stone Fort Entranceway

did mistake the clay for ash, it is almost inconceivable that he could mistake bone and charred vegetable material. We may never know the answer, because the whereabouts of the remains is not known.

The Entranceway: Early Accounts

Every visitor to the Old Stone Fort who has touched his pen to paper has extolled the complex "breastworks" at the front or north side of the structure. One problem, however, is that the visitors do not agree on what they saw. The earliest eyewitnesses describe an entrance much different from the structure drawn by later work-ers. Most writers mention two stone or earth mounds in front of the entranceway and indicate some complexity in construction. Concerning the entrance mounds (or pedestals, as they are some-times called today), Donnison states: "At its northern extremity, and in front of the wall, are two conical pillars of stone, about six feet high, and at the base about 10 or 12 feet in diameter. In the rear of those pillars stands the northern wall extending from one branch of the river to the other" (1819).

The so-called "conical pillars" can still be discerned today, but the details of the entrance found in the following quote from Donnison were not substantiated in later writings, nor were they evident in the excavations of Cox or the 1966 field party. Continuing his description of the entrance complex, Donnison says: "In the northern curtain of the wall is a gateway, which, on this section of the fort, is the only outlet. This wall, on its inner face, is about 10 feet perpendicular. In the rear of the gateway is a stone building, of 16 feet square; on the right of which is one of similar description, of about 10 feet square."

Haywood (1823) reiterates the description of the stone buildings, as do Squire and Davis (1848), who also provide a clearly drawn but obviously incorrect map of the site (Plate 1). It must be remembered that Squire and Davis obtained their information from Haywood, among others. They do, however, mention two plans of the site in the manuscripts of C. S. Rafinesque "which differ slightly from each other" (1848: 31). This certainly indicates that early writers themselves did not agree on the plan of the fort.

One of the first observers to suggest a complex entranceway which would deter easy penetration by intruders or attackers was T. C. Yoakim in 1845. A map accompanying Yoakim's letter is simply executed but shows what seem to be inner walls that parallel each other and a wall meeting these at right angles toward the rear of the entranceway. Yoakim's description of the entrance is very brief, but he stresses the defensive nature of the structure. He says, "I have given a tolerable idea of the entrance which is complex, and seems to have been so constructed as to invite the enemy in that he might be more easily taken." The drawing and description could be interpreted as an attempt to reconstruct the cul-de-sac or "blind alley" entrance first described by Jones in 1876.

Joseph Jones was a first-hand observer and noted that earlier writers were often in error, particularly when describing the entrance. Concerning these earlier accounts, he states: "The account and plan of the Stone Fort given by Squire and Davis, are copied from the 'Western Messenger,' and the errors are due to the writer of the article. In this plan the entrance is especially defective" (1876: 100).

A resurvey of the site by W. A. Thoma of Manchester provided Jones with two plans of the fort—one of the entire structure (Plate 2) and the other of the entrance alone. This latter plan shows two parallel walls extending back from the entrance, the west inner wall being 138 feet in length and the east 120 feet long. The west inner wall makes a 90° turn to the east and continues until parallel with the east inner wall. This forms the so-called back entrance, where there is some suggestion of terminal pillars or mounds at the ends of the walls. Jones (p. 101) describes this cul-de-sac entrance as follows:

> The entrance to the fortification deserves attention. On either side of the main entrance on the north, the wall composed of loose stones has been strengthened, forming what have been described as stone mounds. These more elevated terminations of the wall probably served as lookouts, or positions for defensive stockades and towers. They are about three feet higher than the main wall. Two stone walls extend back from the main entrance, one of which bends at right angles, leaving a space for a back entrance, as represented in Fig. 57.

> The ends of the stone walls facing the main entrance on the inside are enlarged and elevated similarly to those of the outer wall already described. The largest of these foundations for defensive towers, is about sixteen feet square and ten feet high.

Cox's Excavation in the Entranceway

Cox cut only one trench in the cul-de-sac; it was dug through the west alley wall at a distance of 180 feet from the entrance. The excavator stated that the 5 foot wide trench exposed a wall 6 feet 4 inches high, composed almost entirely of shale. Although this trench was apparently the only test in the entrance area, Cox is quite explicit in his description of the features here. It is obvious that Cox did not see the entranceway in its original form since he states, "The greater portion of the inside wall, . . . which is on the east side, has been removed, as I am informed, for the purpose of procuring road material" (1929: 2). His description, then, is probably the result of correlating his observations with the accounts of earlier writers, such as Jones. The only real discrepancy between Cox's and Jones's accounts is in details about the back entrance of the cul-de-sac. Although both writers agree that small conical structures were found at the east end of the inner walls, Cox states that "*both* [emphasis mine] inside walls turn abruptly to the left (east), extend a distance of about eighty feet and terminate in two small conical structures, of the same material, on the extreme eastern end of the last described wall" (1929: 2).

1966 Excavations in the Entranceway

Twelve excavation units—nine trenches and three test pits—were placed in the entrance complex at strategic points (see Figure 6).

Trench 7—This trench was dug across the end of the west entrance wall. The 5 feet wide by 45.4 feet long unit was excavated to a depth of only 0.5 feet, exposing a fill composed almost entirely of rock.

Trench 8—In the almost destroyed east entrance wall a trench was dug to determine the original width of the wall base and the amount of erosional deposit from both entrance walls. Trench 8 was 5 feet wide and 67.1 feet long, extending across the former east entrance wall and into the base of the west entrance wall. There was some indication that the east entrance wall was not as wide as the west entrance wall.

Trench 9—This was a 5 feet wide by 27.9 feet long trench cut into the outer face of the west entrance wall where that wall makes a sharp turn to the east. Only 0.5 feet of humus was removed along the length of the trench; the wall here was composed mainly of rubble.

Trench 10—A trench was excavated from the apex of the west pedestal to the north end of the west entrance wall. This 5 feet wide by 30.9 feet long excavation both tested the composition of the west pedestal and verified that the pedestal and west entrance wall had never been connected. The first indication of a ditch (Feature

4) was apparent in this trench between the pedestal and entrance wall. Here the ditch had been filled with stacked rock; a 3 by 5 foot test section of this ditch indicated that the stacked rock reached a depth of 4.9 feet.

Trench 11—This test in the west entrance wall was a re-excavation of the southwest profile of Cox's Trench 4. Cox implies that the wall was constructed merely by indiscriminate piling of shale and broken "flint," but the re-excavation proved the existence of incipient inner and outer walls constructed of chert and shale with a fill between them of primarily shale, with some earth. The profile showed that the height of the west entrance wall here is 5.3 feet.

Trench 12—A 3 feet wide by 23.7 feet long trench was dug down the outer face of the west entrance wall and extended 18 feet beyond the edge of the embankment. The humus was stripped away to expose the rock construction.

Trench 13—This trench was dug across the rear opening of the cul-de-sac. The 3 feet wide by 17.2 feet long excavation exposed 3.4 feet of the south end of the east entrance wall. The wall fill was, as usual, rock chunks. Although it was difficult to determine the exact opening, at this point the rear entrance was 15.9 feet wide.

Trench 14—This 5 feet wide by 20 feet long trench was placed in the center of the alleyway between the two entrance walls to see whether the ditch evident in Trench 10 and Test Pit 14 (see below) extended across the entrance. It was discovered that the ditch had extended across the entrance. On each side, stacked rock had been placed in the ditch between the pedestal and the end of the entrance wall. This ditch was designated Feature 4.

Trench 14 indicates that the ditch was originally 4.3 feet deep; at that depth the cherty bedrock was encountered. Scattered charcoal and an area of fire-reddened clay was found in the bottom of the ditch, and a charcoal sample was collected for dating (see page 24). Flint chipping debris and a broken projectile point found near the bottom of this feature suggest that this portion of the ditch remained open for some time. The stacked rock at either side of the entrance probably prevented wash from the other portion of the ditch, which might have been filled after the entrance complex was

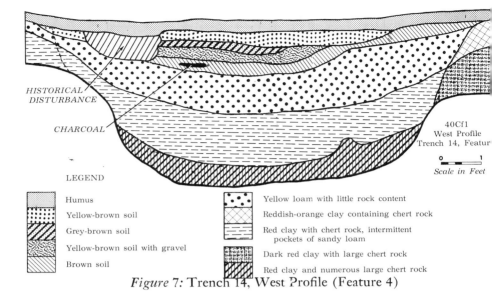

HISTORICAL
DISTURBANCE

CHARCOAL

40Cf1
West Profile
Trench 14, Featur

0   1
Scale in Feet

LEGEND

▦ Humus	⦁⦁⦁ Yellow loam with little rock content
▦ Yellow-brown soil	⊠ Reddish-orange clay containing chert rock
▨ Grey-brown soil	≡ Red clay with chert rock, intermittent pockets of sandy loam
▧ Yellow-brown soil with gravel	▦ Dark red clay with large chert rock
▨ Brown soil	▨ Red clay and numerous large chert rock

Figure 7: Trench 14, West Profile (Feature 4)

built. The northwest profile of the ditch (see Figure 7) suggests that the ditch was originally 10.4 feet wide at the top and 6.3 feet wide at the base. This tapering was probably partially due to erosion into the ditch, especially from the north or entrance side. Or, possibly the ditch was deliberately filled with the layers of red clay and yellowish loam seen in the northwest profile.

Trench 16—The southeast side of the west pedestal was tested with a 3 feet wide by 12.6 feet long trench which showed that here the pedestal was built almost entirely of earth.

Test Pit 13—This was a 16 feet wide by 16 feet long test block dug on the west side of the east pedestal. Again, the excavated portion of the pedestal was constructed primarily of earth.

Test Pit 14—This was a 3 feet wide by 5 feet long test pit excavated between the west pedestal and entrance wall. Like the 3 by 5 foot section of Trench 10, this unit revealed stacked rock in the entrance ditch (Feature 4). The rock extended to a depth of 5.7 feet.

Test Pit 15—A 12 feet wide by 13.6 feet long block was dug on the north slope of the east pedestal. This excavation confirmed the earth fill discovered in Test Pit 13.

Conclusions about the Entranceway

Only one gateway is evident in the outer walls today, this being in the front or north wall. Although early writers such as Donnison mention a gateway in the south wall, later observers such as Jones do not indicate its presence. The only known opening in this embankment before Cox's Test Trench 3 was a cut for a wagon road at the southwestern side of the enclosure; a back entranceway might have originally been located at this cut. There is no evidence of such a gateway elsewhere in the wall. Considering the complexity of the front entrance, it seems unlikely that a mere gap would have been left as an entrance in the long back or south wall.

The front entrance with its elaborate earth and stone "breastworks" has been a favorite topic for many writers, and the remaining "battlements" still suggest a plan for defense. Unfortunately, these reports do not agree on the configuration of these works. For this reason a major portion of the 1966 field season was spent in the entrance complex.

Since the early writers disagree greatly concerning the entrance complex, some must have been in error. Among the most glaring inconsistencies are a failure to mention the parallel walls of the cul-de-sac and a description of two enigmatic "stone houses" inside the front entrance.

The 1966 excavations in the entrance complex prove definitely that Donnison's early account is in error; therefore the reports of Haywood and of Squire and Davis, which are based on Donnison's account, are also in error. Even if the 1966 excavations had not been so conclusive, the present west entrance wall proves the existence of an entrance passageway which, strangely, Donnison does not mention. There is no indication that two "stone buildings" ever existed inside the front wall, but perhaps these structures were not a figment of Donnison's imagination; the two pedestals at the inner ends of the two cul-de-sac walls could have been mistaken for "buildings," particularly if they were somewhat flat on top. Unfortunately, these two pedestals have been destroyed, so this interpretation cannot be proved. In any case, the

Figure 8: Sketch of Entranceway

other details discovered in the 1966 excavations indicate that Jones's description and plan of the fort are probably the most nearly accurate.

We can now present a tentative sketch of the construction procedures and details in the north entranceway (Figure 8). One of the most important discoveries was the definite presence of a ditch across at least a portion of the narrow neck of the ridge. Whether this ditch was made at the time the outer walls were built is not known, but it is obviously earlier than at least a part of the entrance complex since a portion of the end of the cul-de-sac walls overlapped the stone fill in the ditch. The original extent of this ditch is not known.

When completed, the entranceway probably had the following configuration. Two conical pillars or pedestals stood on opposite sides of the main entrance. Today these pedestals are 24 feet apart. The east pedestal is smaller, with a diameter of 35 feet and a height of 5 feet. The west pedestal is 48 feet in diameter and 6 feet in height. These pedestals were connected to the front or north outer wall, which is now almost totally destroyed. Unlike most of that wall, the pedestals are composed primarily of earth. They were not connected to the parallel or cul-de-sac walls, although they were aligned with those walls. Between the pedestals and the entrance walls was the ditch, which was modified to meet the demands of a more complex gateway. Rock was stacked in the ditch only between the pedestals and the entrance walls. Because those open portions of the ditch on either side of the alleyway of the cul-de-sac and entranceway would have been inside the front wall and therefore useless, they were probably refilled with earth. The rock was stacked in the ditch between the pedestals and the entrance walls to keep this fill from washing into the portion of the ditch that remained open across the entrance.

The east and west parallel walls of the cul-de-sac were apparently constructed after this modification of the ditch. Trench 8 indicates that the distance between the east and west walls was about 20 feet. The six test trenches dug completely or partially into the west entrance wall and the re-excavation of Cox's Trench 4 indicate that this embankment was constructed like the outer walls. Trench 11 revealed what could be inner and outer inclusive walls composed primarily of chert with a "filler" between containing more shale and some earth. These tests also showed little erosion, suggesting that the west cul-de-sac wall, at least, is still close to its original height of less than six feet. The length of the west entrance wall is 214 feet, including the 54 feet of back entrance wall that forms the cul-de-sac. Thus, the actual west wall of the alleyway is 160 feet long, considerably more than Jones's measurement of 138 feet (1876: Figure 57).

The two trenches placed across the almost destroyed east entrance wall did not conclusively determine the construction or former size of this wall, but they suggested that this wall had a narrower base than the west wall. This might indicate that the east wall was lower than the west wall. Traceable rubble shows that the east entrance wall was at least 112 feet long; Jones indicates a total length of 120 feet (1876: Figure 57).

Although the back entrance wall of the cul-de-sac was destroyed with the east entrance wall, two test trenches placed across the former opening between the walls indicated that Jones's drawing of this entrance is probably correct. He shows the east end of the west entrance wall and the south end of the parallel east wall almost meeting, to form an entrance 18 feet wide (1876: Figure 57). Cox's observation that both entrance walls turn to the east (1929: 2) does not seem to be correct. Besides substantiating Jones's gen-

eral description of the rear entrance, the 1966 tests suggested that
this entrance was about 16 feet wide. No evidence of the rear
pillars or pedestals described by Jones was discovered.

The Enclosed Area: Early Accounts

Donnison (1819) again provides us with the earliest description
of the area enclosed by the walls. This writer states that the interior area was partially plowed in 1819. When the area was first
cultivated, Donnison says: "They ploughed up a fine piece of flint
glass, about one inch in thickness, and of remarkable transparency
—it appears to have been a piece of bowl—was neatly polished and
fluted on its sides. At the same time was found a small stone, very
beautifully carved and ornamented, much superior to any known
art of the Indians."

Although the early ground-breaking within the walls might have
produced artifacts related to the builders, Jones's search of this
area for some evidence of aboriginal occupation seems to set the
pace for later tests in this area. Jones states: "I carefully searched
the enclosure for stone graves and relics, but discovered nothing
relating to the aborigines. As the fort had been used by soldiers
during a portion of the recent war (1861–65) for a camping
ground, and as a mill had been erected on the Barren Fork, fragments of iron utensils and of copper are occasionally found, also
lead bullets, but these are clearly of modern date" (1876: 101–
102).

Cox was the first to test the inner area by sinking test pits and
trenches below the plow-disturbed ground. During his two weeks
of excavation, more than sixty test pits and "numbers" of trenches
were excavated in a ten-acre corn field and in the uncultivated section covered with weeds and grass. These tests were entirely in-
conclusive, as Cox (1929: 3) reveals:

> As to the area inside the walls there is a total absence of any
> evidence of habitation or temporary occupancy as is usually in-
> dicated by fire, ashes, burned floors, fragments, building material,
> animal bones, pottery or other implements or utensils, for defense,
> offense, or domestic purposes. There was a total absence of any
> evidence of burial in this area, usually indicated by stone graves

and human bones, although within easy reach were tons of shale slabs of the kind used as material for constructing stone graves.

1966 Excavations of the Enclosed Area

In 1966, twelve 3 by 3 foot hand-excavated test pits and about eighty-five mechanically excavated trenches were strategically placed inside the walls to find areas of occupation that previous workers might have missed. Although a few scattered artifacts and some flint chips were recovered, no evidence of permanent occupation was discovered. One important result of these tests, however, was the revelation that buried humus lines disappear rapidly in the acid soil. A test trench dug on the site of an old farm house showed a barely discernible humus line. This might be the reason no buried humus lines were discovered under the walls and no organic material was present in the wall fill. This also might account for the absence of bone in the enclosure, but it does not explain the rarity of stone artifacts and absence of such features as fire basins and pits. Unless subsequent testing uncovers evidence to the contrary, Cox's opinion (1929: 8) that "[The Old Stone Fort] was constructed for temporary . . . purposes, as distinguished from permanent occupancy as a habitation site" may indeed stand.

The Moat, or Ditch

Although no effort was made in the 1966 field season to test the so-called "moat" extending between the two streams below the south end of the enclosure, no report on the Old Stone Fort would be complete without some comment on this feature. This "moat" has always been mentioned as an integral defensive unit of the "fort," Donnison (1819) describing it as follows: "On the south side of the south curtain of this fort, there is at the base of the wall a ditch of about 16 or 20 feet in width, extending from river to river. Here also appears to have been an immense excavation of earth; the average breadth is from 80 to 100 feet, and about 40 feet in depth, extending from river to river, at the bottom of which, and next to the wall, is the ditch." What Donnison saw might have been a natural channel—his "immense excavation of earth"—deepened by an artificial ditch. The ditch, filled with water from the two streams, would have served as a defensive moat.

54

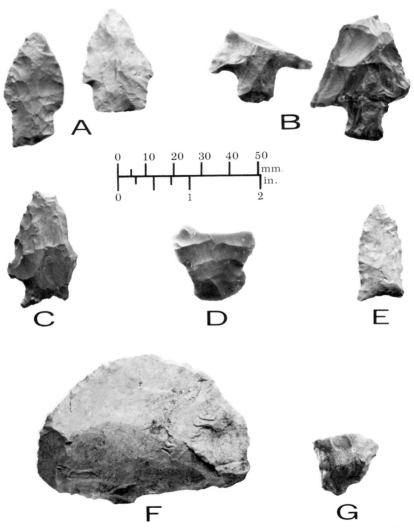

Plate 13: Chipped Stone Artifacts: A–Straight-stemmed, narrow blade; B–Straight-stemmed, wide blade; C–Expanded-stemmed; D–Adena; E–Large triangular; F–Side scraper; G–End scraper.

Later descriptions of this ditch are less emphatic about its artificial origin. Jones states that the ditch "is supposed to have been designed to convey water across" (1876: 101), and Cox says that excavation had proved that the ditch "had been an artificial water course" (1929: 8), but does not elaborate. The 1966 investigators, too, had doubts about this being a man-made feature. The wide channel between the rivers is probably a former stream bed connecting the two forks. Whether the builders of the enclosure modified this channel so that water would flow through it at all times cannot be proved at the present. Such a moat might be unprecedented among North American prehistoric enclosures or fortifications. A writer on primitive warfare states, "I know of no use of a water curtain, that is, a moat, among any nonliterate peoples" (Turney-High, 1949: 17). Only extensive excavation will indicate the natural or artificial nature of this channel.

Artifacts Recovered in the 1966 Excavations

Although aboriginal artifacts were recovered in the walls and in the interior of the enclosure, none of these could be definitely ascribed to the builders of the structure. It is certain that artifacts found deep within the walls or at the bottom of the entrance ditch could date no later than these walls or the ditch, but they could indeed be much earlier. The only conclusion that can be drawn about cultural remains in the Old Stone Fort must be based on their infrequent occurrence. The absence or small number of certain utilitarian items indicates either that the site was never used intensively for habitation or that these things were deliberately removed.

Although a number of 19th and 20th century items were recovered in the humus layer in scattered portions of the site, this collection (including metal, porcelain, glass, etc.) can be ascribed to the industrial activity in this area during the 19th century, its use as a bivouac area during the Civil War, and sojourns to this site by 20th century picnickers and other pleasure seekers. Thus we can bid adieu to this debris and turn to the few artifacts that pertain to prehistoric visitations to this site.

The aboriginal artifacts recovered on the site are listed in Tables

56

TABLE 2: DISTRIBUTION OF PROJECTILE POINTS

Provenience	Adena	Straight-stemmed, narrow blade	Straight-stemmed, wide blade	Expanded-stemmed	Large triangular	Total
Feat. 4, Tr. 14 3.55' B.S.*	1	–	–	–	–	1
Tr. 2 1.5'–2.0' B.S.	–	–	–	1	–	1
Tr. 3 0.0'–0.5' B.S.	–	–	2	–	–	2
Tr. 8 0.5'–1.0' B.S.	–	–	–	–	1	1
T. P. 13 0.5'–1.0' B.S.	–	2	–	–	–	2
Total	1	2	2	1	1	(7)

*Below surface

2 and 3. Besides a dearth of worked lithic tools, the infrequency of flakes and cores is especially notable. Except for a concentration of flint chips in the bottom of Feature 4, the entrance ditch, there is little evidence of workshop activity on the site. Concerning the chips in Feature 4, it appears that a flint knapper sat near the edge of the ditch while striking flakes from a large core, the waste flakes being thrown into the ditch. The distal end of a projectile point and a side scraper were found in the humus layer above the ditch. The other tools found in the trenches and test pits include a uniface end scraper (Plate 13, G) and a large flake with a longitudinal working edge that shows some retouch (Plate 13, F). While these two items could be Paleo-Indian artifacts, the remainder of the tools such as biface scrapers, flake spokeshaves, and the chert hammerstones listed in Table 3 is typical of either the Archaic or Woodland periods.

TABLE 3: DISTRIBUTION OF CHIPPED STONE ARTIFACTS

Provenience	Projectile Points Broken, Unidentified	Spokeshaves	Side Scrapers	End Scrapers	Cores	Chert Hammerstone	Unidentified Worked Flint	Utilized Flakes	Unworked Flint	Total
Trench 1	–	1	–	–	1	–	3	29	138	172
Trench 2	1	–	2	–	–	1	–	4	87	95
Trench 3	1	–	–	1	1	–	3	13	64	83
Trench 5	–	–	2	–	–	–	–	5	15	22
Trench 6	–	–	–	–	–	–	2	1	–	3
Trench 7	–	–	–	–	–	–	–	4	16	20
Trench 8	1	–	1	2	–	1	1	5	21	32
Trench 9	–	–	–	–	–	–	–	2	12	14
Trench 10	–	–	–	–	–	–	–	6	9	15
Trench 11	–	–	–	–	–	–	1	–	1	2
Trench 12	–	–	–	–	–	–	–	1	3	4
Trench 13	–	–	–	–	–	–	2	2	16	20
Trench 15	–	–	1	–	–	–	–	1	8	10
Test Pit 4	–	–	–	–	–	–	–	1	19	20
Test Pit 6	–	–	–	–	–	–	2	3	10	15
Test Pit 7	1	–	–	–	–	–	–	2	14	17
Test Pit 12	–	–	–	–	–	–	–	1	–	1
Test Pit 13	–	–	1	–	–	–	–	15	30	46
Test Pit 15	–	–	–	–	–	–	–	2	19	21
Feature 4	1	–	1	–	–	–	–	15	594	611
Total	5	1	8	3	2	2	14	112	1076	(1223)

Seven identifiable projectile points were recovered during the excavation (Table 2 and Plate 13), but these can be only ascribed to either the Archaic or Woodland periods, and none can be positively associated with the Middle Woodland builders of the enclosure. One broken stemmed projectile point (Plate 13, D) with a ground stem and bold flaking appears to be an Adena type (Bell, 1958: 4–5). The artifact was found at a depth of 3.55 feet in the entrance ditch, and had to be deposited while the ditch was still open. This is probably an Early Woodland artifact. Another Woodland projectile point is the triangular or stemless point found in Trench 8 (Plate 13, E). The other stemmed projectile points (Plate 13, A-C) could be either Late Archaic or Early Woodland artifacts, and probably pre-date the enclosure.

The most obviously missing artifact in this list of objects found in the Old Stone Fort is pottery. We know that the prehistoric cultures which might have built this enclosure were using pottery by the time the walls were raised, and there are three possible explanations for its absence in the area. One is that our particular excavation units just happened to be in areas where sherds were not deposited (*i.e.*, sampling error); the second is that the builders did not use many pottery vessels at this site; the third is that the site was carefully cleaned after use. Since the 1966 investigations involved more than twenty large excavation units, the last two possibilities seem more likely than sampling error. Pottery vessels are usually associated with specific activities of females; therefore the absence of pottery on this site suggests that the principal maintenance and ceremonial activities were carried out by males. The presence of chipping debris in Feature 4 further indicates predominant male activity here since stone tool making is usually a male task. As discussed above in the section on the function of the site, either of these two explanations would support a "ceremonial" theory of the function of the Old Stone Fort.

∽ SUMMARY ∾

WE CAN NOW make several substantive statements about the Old Stone Fort and related enclosure sites in the eastern United States. Although unanswered questions still remain, the 1966 excavation provided the following information:

1) Some early descriptions of the Old Stone Fort are of dubious value from the point of view of interpretation and reconstruction. The most accurate description of the enclosure was made by Jones in 1876.

2) The entranceway and internal construction of the walls are similar to constructions found in some Ohio hilltop enclosures that were built by the Ohio Hopewell culture. There is strong evidence that the Old Stone Fort was built by an as yet archaeologically undefined local Middle Woodland culture that was related to both Ohio Hopewell and neighboring Hopewell-influenced groups in the Southeast such as Copena and Marksville.

3) The Old Stone Fort was built over a period of three or four hundred years in the first centuries of the Christian Era. The dates for the Old Stone Fort compare favorably with the radiocarbon date for Miami Fort and the estimated age for other Hopewell hilltop enclosures in Ohio.

4) There is no evidence that the Old Stone Fort ever served as a habitation site for its builders. The few artifacts found during the excavation indicate earlier people lived on the site, but none of the artifacts recovered can be definitely attributed to its builders.

5) Although there is no evidence of ceremonial activity within the walls of the Old Stone Fort, the large area encompassed by the walls, the apparent absence of a palisade to reinforce the low walls, and the scarcity of habitation debris inside the walls suggest a

ceremonial rather than a defensive function. The stone mounds in the vicinity of some of these enclosures in the Southeast were possibly built at the same time as the enclosures although a lack of field data prevents a more positive correlation between the two. The same neglect of enclosure sites prevents us from stating that all enclosure sites in the eastern United States had the same function or were even built at the same time; however, the above features of the Old Stone Fort and other similar enclosures suggest they were ceremonial centers rather than defensive forts. One of the unanswered questions that remains is what kind of ceremony took place at these sites? Hopefully, further excavation will answer this question.

❦ REFERENCES ❧

ATWATER, CALEB
1820 "Description of the Antiquities Discovered in the State of Ohio and Other Western States." *American Antiquarian Society, Archaeologia Americana, Transactions, and Collections*, Vol. 1, pp. 105–267. Worchester, Massachusetts.

BABY, RAYMOND S.
1966a Personal communication, August 13.
1966b Letter to author, December 12.

BELL, ROBERT E.
1958 *Guide to the Identification of Certain American Indian Projectile Points*. Special Bulletin No. 1 of the Oklahoma Anthropological Society. Oklahoma City.

BROADHEAD, G. C.
1880 "Prehistoric Evidences in Missouri." *Annual Report of the Smithsonian Institution for 1879*, pp. 350–59. Washington, D.C.

CHAPMAN, CARL H.
1947 "A Preliminary Survey of Missouri Archaeology, Part II: Middle Mississippi and Hopewellian Cultures." *Missouri Archaeologist*, Vol. 10, Pt. II, pp. 61–94. Columbia.
1953 "The Archaeological Survey of Missouri." *Missouri Archaeologist*, Vol. 15, Nos. 1–2, pp. 7–41. Columbia.

COX, P. E.
1929 "Preliminary Report of Exploration at Old Stone Fort, Manchester, Tennessee." *Journal of the Tennessee Academy of Science*, Vol. 4, No. 1, pp. 1–7. Nashville.

DAVIDSON, DONALD
1946 *The Tennessee, Vol. I: The Old River, Frontier to Secession.* New York.

DONNISON, WILLIAM
1819 "American Antiquities in Tennessee," letter (to Samuel L. Mitchell of New York) in *The Columbian Centinel,* July 31, 1819. Boston.

DRIVER, HAROLD E.
1961 *Indians of North America.* Chicago.

EWELL, LEIGHTON
1936 *History of Coffee County, Tennessee.* Manchester, Tennessee.

FAULKNER, CHARLES H.
1967 "Tennessee Radiocarbon Dates." *Tennessee Archaeologist,* Vol. 23, No. 1, pp. 12–30. Knoxville.

FISCHER, FRED W., AND C. H. McNUTT
1962 "Test Excavations at Pinson Mounds, 1961." *Tennessee Archaeologist,* Vol. 18, No. 1, pp. 1–13. Knoxville.

FORD, JAMES A.
1951 *Greenhouse: A Troyville-Coles Creek Period Site in Avoyelles Parish, Louisiana.* Anthropological Papers of the American Museum of Natural History, Vol. 44, Pt. 1. New York.

FOWKE, GERARD
1902 *Archaeological History of Ohio.* Columbus.
1910 *Antiquities of Central and Southeastern Missouri.* Bureau of American Ethnology, Bulletin No. 37. Washington, D.C.
1928 "Archaeological Investigations—II: Explorations in the Red River Valley in Louisiana." *Forty-Fourth Annual Report, Bureau of American Ethnology, 1926–1927,* pp. 405–540. Washington, D.C.

FUNKHOUSER, W. D., AND WILLIAM S. WEBB
1928 *Ancient Life in Kentucky.* Kentucky Geological Survey, Series 6, Vol. 34. Frankfort.
1932 *Archaeological Survey of Kentucky.* The University of

Kentucky Reports in Archaeology and Anthropology, Vol. 2. Lexington.

GRIFFIN, JAMES B.
1958 "The Chronological Position of the Hopewellian Culture in the Eastern United States." *Museum of Anthropology Anthropological Papers*, No. 12. Ann Arbor.

HAYWOOD, JOHN
1823 *The Natural and Aboriginal History of Tennessee up to the First Settlements therein by the White People in the year 1768.* 1959 edition edited by Mary U. Rothrock. Jackson, Tennessee.

INGRAM, JOSEPH W., SIGFUS OLAFSON, AND EDWARD V. MCMICHAEL
1961 "The Mount Carbon Walls: Description and History." *West Virginia Archeologist*, No. 13, pp. 1–13. Moundsville.

JENNINGS, JESSE D.
1946 "Hopewell-Copena Sites Near Nashville." *American Antiquity*, Vol. 12, No. 2, p. 126. Menasha, Wisconsin.

JONES, JOSEPH
1876 *Explorations of the Aboriginal Remains of Tennessee.* Smithsonian Contributions to Knowledge 259. Washington, D.C.

KELLAR, JAMES H.
1960 *The C. L. Lewis Stone Mound and the Stone Mound Problem.* Indiana Historical Society, Prehistoric Research Series, Vol. 3, No. 4. Indianapolis.
1961 "Excavations at Mound Carbon, West Virginia." *West Virginia Archeologist*, No. 13, pp. 14–18. Moundsvillle.

LILLY, ELI, C. F. VOEGELIN, ERMINIE W. VOEGELIN, JOE E. PIERCE, PAUL WEER, GLENN A. BLACK, AND GEORG K. NEUMANN
1954 *Walam Olum or Red Score: The Migration Legend of the Lenni Lenape or Delaware Indians.* Indianapolis.

LOVE, T. R., L. D. WILLIAMS, W. H. PROFITT, I. B. EPLEY, AND JOHN ELDER
1959 *Soil Survey of Coffee County, Tennessee.* United States

Department of Agriculture, Series 1956, No. 5. Washington, D.C.

McMAHAN, BASIL B.

1965 *The Mystery of the Old Stone Fort.* Nashville.

MILLS, WILLIAM C.

1906 "Baum Prehistoric Village." *Ohio State Archaeological and Historical Quarterly*, Vol. 15, pp. 45–136. Columbus.

1916 "Exploration of the Tremper Mound." *Ohio State Archaeological and Historical Quarterly*, Vol. 25, pp. 263–398. Columbus.

MOOREHEAD, WARREN K.

1890 *Fort Ancient.* Cincinnati.

1932 "Exploration of the Etowah Site in Georgia." *Etowah Papers.* Department of Archaeology, Phillips Academy, Andover, Massachusetts. New Haven.

MORGAN, RICHARD G.

1946 *Fort Ancient.* The Ohio State Archaeological and Historical Society. Columbus.

1952 "Outline of Cultures in the Ohio Region." *Archeology of Eastern United States*, edited by James B. Griffin, pp. 83–98. Chicago.

MORGAN, RICHARD G., AND E. S. THOMAS

1948 *Fort Hill.* Ohio State Archaeological and Historical Society. Columbus.

MORSE, DAN F., AND JAMES H. POLHEMUS, III

n.d. *Preliminary Investigations of the Pinson Mounds Site Near Jackson, Tennessee.* Unpublished Field Report on file in the Department of Anthropology, University of Tennessee. Knoxville.

MYER, WILLIAM E.

1928 "Indian Trails of the Southeast," edited by J. R. Swanton. *Forty-Second Annual Report, Bureau of American Ethnology, 1924–1925*, pp. 727–857. Washington, D.C.

PRUFER, OLAF H.

1964 "The Hopewell Complex of Ohio." *Hopewellian Studies*, Illinois State Museum Scientific Papers, Vol. 12, pp. 35–83. Springfield.

PUTNAM, FREDRICK W.

1882 "Notes on Copper Objects from North and South America, Contained in the Collections of the Peabody Museum." *Fifteenth Annual Report of the Peabody Museum of American Archaeology and Ethnology*, Vol. 3, No. 2, pp. 83–148. Cambridge, Massachusetts.

ROBERTS, RALPH G.

1949 "Ancient Stone Fortifications at De Soto Falls, Little River, Alabama." *Tennessee Archaeologist*, Vol. 5, No. 2, pp. 18–21. Knoxville.

ROWE, JOHN H.

1946 "Inca Culture at the Time of the Spanish Conquest." *Handbook of South American Indians*, edited by Julian H. Steward, Vol. 2, pp. 183–330. Bureau of American Ethnology, Bulletin 143, Smithsonian Institution, Washington, D.C.

SEARS, WILLIAM H.

1961 "The Study of Social and Religious Systems in North American Archaeology." *Current Anthropology*, Vol. 2, No. 3, pp. 223–31. Chicago.

SHETRONE, HENRY C.

1930 *The Mound Builders*. New York.

SHETRONE, HENRY C., AND E. F. GREENMAN

1931 "Explorations of the Seip Group of Prehistoric Earthworks." *Ohio State Archaeological and Historical Quarterly*, Vol. 40, No. 3, pp. 349–509. Columbus.

SMITH, PHILLIP E.

1962 "Aboriginal Stone Constructions in the Southern Piedmont." *University of Georgia Laboratory of Archaeology Series*, Report No. 4, pp. 1–47. Athens.

SPETH, JOHN D.

1966 "The Whorley Earthwork." *Edge Area Archaeology*, edited by James E. Fitting. *Michigan Archaeologist*, Vol. 12, No. 4, pp. 211–27. Ann Arbor.

SQUIRE, EPHRAIM G., AND EDWIN H. DAVIS

1848 *Ancient Monuments of the Mississippi Valley*. Smithsonian Contributions to Knowledge, Vol. 1. Washington, D.C.

STRUEVER, STUART

   1965 "Middle Woodland Culture History in the Great Lakes Riverine Area." *American Antiquity*, Vol. 31, No. 2, Pt. 1, pp. 211–23. Salt Lake City.

THRUSTON, GATES P.

   1897 *The Antiquities of Tennessee*. Cincinnati.

TURNEY-HIGH, HARRY H.

   1949 *Primitive War*. Columbia, South Carolina.

WARING, A. J., JR.

   1945 " 'Hopewellian' Elements in Northern Georgia." *American Antiquity*, Vol. 11, No. 2, pp. 119–20. Menasha, Wisconsin.

WEBB, WILLIAM S.

   1939 *An Archaeological Survey of Wheeler Basin on the Tennessee River in Northern Alabama*. Bureau of American Ethnology, Bulletin 122. Washington, D.C.

WHITTLESEY, CHARLES

   1883 "The Great Mound on the Etowah River, Georgia." *Annual Report of the Smithsonian Institution for 1881*, pp. 624–30. Washington, D.C.

WITTHOFT, JOHN

   1949 *Green Corn Ceremonialism in the Eastern Woodlands*. Occasional Contributions from the Museum of Anthropology of the University of Michigan, No. 13. Ann Arbor.

YOAKIM, T. C.

   1845 Letter dated Murfreesboro, Tennessee, July 25, 1845.

YOUNG, BENNETT H.

   1910 *The Prehistoric Men of Kentucky*. Louisville.

ᥴᕉ INDEX ᕉᥴ

Entranceways: complex, 3, 8, 11, 13, 16, 17, 24, 25, 27, 28, 30, 44, 45, 46, 47, 48, 49
Erwin, Colonel Andrew: on Old Stone Fort, 34

Ford, James A.: on village plazas, 31. *See also* Function, ceremonial
Fort Ancient, 11, 13, 14, 18, 22, 29, 30
Fort Hill, 12, 30–31
Fort Miami, 26, 59
Fort Payne chert, 1, 2
Fortified Hill, 12, 13, 14
Fowke, Gerard: on defensive function, 27; on Old Fort, 16–17, 18; on Spruce Hill, 13
Franklin, Tenn.: mound near, 21
Franquelin, Jean Baptiste Louis, 31–32
Function: ceremonial, 11, 14, 28, 29, 30, 31, 32, 58, 59–60; defensive, 10, 26, 27, 28, 29, 42, 44

Galena, 21, 22
Geochron Laboratories, 23–24
Georgia: enclosure sites in, 15, 16, 18; mounds in, 18–19
Green Corn ceremony, 31
Greenhouse site, 31
Greenstone. *See* Celts
Gulf Coast: trade with Ohio Valley, 31

Haywood, Judge John: on Old Stone Fort, 8, 23
Highland Rim, 1
Hopewell culture: 10, 11, 18, 19, 20, 21, 22, 23, 25, 28, 30, 31, 59; age of, 25; artifacts of, 20; burial mounds of, 20, 21; settlement pattern of, 20–21; trade in, 31. *See also* Middle Woodland period

Ice Age, 9
Incas, 29

Jones, Joseph: on Old Stone Fort, 8, 19, 34, 41, 49–50, 51–52, 55, 59; on Squire and Davis, 44–45

Kentucky: enclosure sites in, 15, 16, 17

Ladd Mountain enclosure, 15, 16, 18
La Salle, Robert Cavelier, Sieur de, 31
Late Woodland period, 10. *See also* Tennessee
Lebanon, Tenn.: mound near, 21
Lenni Lenape, 29
Little Duck River, 6

McMahan, Basil B., 9
Madoc, Prince, 9
Manchester, Tenn., 1, 8, 19, 45
Marksville culture, 19, 23, 59
Marshall County, Tenn.: artifacts found in, 21; mounds in, 21
Mica, 18
Michigan: enclosure sites in, 31
Middle Woodland period: 10, 17, 21, 22, 23, 25, 32, 59; burials in 18; pan-regional trade in, 23. *See also* Hopewell culture; Tennessee
Mississippian period, 9. *See also* Tennessee
Missouri: enclosure sites in, 15, 16, 17, 18, 30
Moorehead, Warren K.: on Fort Ancient, 11, 12, 14
Morgan, Richard G.: on ceremonial function, 28, 29–30
Mound Builders, 9
Mounds: burial, 10, 11, 18, 19, 21, 22, 29, 30; entrance, 6, 11, 13, 14,

Spruce Hill, 12, 13
Squire, Ephraim G. *See* Squire and Davis
Squire and Davis: on defensive function, 27; on Fortified Hill, 12, 13; on mounds and earthworks in Ohio, 10; on Old Stone Fort, 8
Steatite. *See* Pipes
Stone constructions. *See* Southeastern United States

Tennessee: Indian trails in, 31–32; mounds in, 19, 21; prehistoric periods in, 9, 10
Tennessee River, 21, 22
Thoma, W. A.: early survey of Old Stone Fort, 45
Tlascalan gateways, 13. *See also* Fortified Hill
Trade, 31
Trails, Indian, 31–32
Tremper mound, 21
Troyville-Coles Creek period, 31
Turney-High, Harry H.: on defensive moats, 55; on Indian warfare, 28

Walls: destruction of, 1, 40–41, 50; height of, 28, 33, 34, 35, 36, 39, 40, 44, 45, 51; inclusive, 35, 36, 39, 42, 51; length of, 3, 6, 8, 51. *See also* Old Stone Fort
—De Soto Falls, 15, 16, 17
—Fort Mountain, 15, 16
—Indian Fort Mountain, 15, 16, 17
—Mount Carbon, 15, 17, 18
—Sand Mountain, 15–16, 18
Webb, William S.: on reel-shaped gorgets, 21–22
Western Messenger, 8
West Virginia: enclosure sites in, 15, 17, 18; mounds in, 18
Whorley Earthwork, 31
Williamson County, Tenn.: artifacts found in, 21; mounds in, 21
Witthoft, John: on Busk ceremony, 31
Woodland period: 9, 10, 17, 21, 22, 23, 25, 32, 56, 57. *See also* Tennessee

Yoakim, T. C.: on Old Stone Fort, 34, 41, 44
Yuchi, 9

DATE DUE

The Old Stone Fort has been set on the Linotype in eleven point Janson with two-point spacing between the lines. Hadriano No. 309 and Hadriano Stone Cut were selected for display.

THE UNIVERSITY OF TENNESSEE PRESS: KNOXVILLE